Presented To

_____

From

_____

Date

_____

GOD'S ROAD WARRIOR

GOD'S ROAD WARRIOR

ARE YOU GOING MY WAY?

Frank Barrera

Copyright 2014 – Frank Barrera

All rights reserved. This book is protected by the copyright laws of the United States of America. This book may not be copied or reprinted or commercial gain or profit. The use of short quotations or occasional page copying for personal use is permitted and encouraged. Permission will be granted upon request.

Unless otherwise indicated, all Scripture quotations are taken from *The New King James Version of the Bible,* Copyright © 1979, 1980 by Tomas Nelson, Inc., Publishers. Used by permission.

Drawbaugh Publishing Group
444 Allen Drive
Chambersburg, PA 17202

Paperback ISBN: 978-1-941746-09-7

eBookISBN: 978-1-941746-10-3

For worldwide Distribution, Printed in the United States.

1 2 3 4 5 6 7 8 9 10 / 16 15 14

Table of Contents

Preface.. ix
Acknowledgements xiii

Chapter 1 – *"Junk-Drawer"* 1

Chapter 2 – *Another Delay* 9

Chapter 3 – *Signs* 17

Chapter 4 – *Pulled Over* 29

Chapter 5 – *The Cardboard Sign Read –
          Homeless* 39

Chapter 6 – *Problem or Inconvenience* 47

Chapter 7 – *Long Night in Loon Lodge* 55

Chapter 8 – *And the Sky is not Cloudy All-Day* 63

Chapter 9 – *Grateful* 75

Chapter 10 – *Outside Rider on an Inside Road* 89

Chapter 11 – *The Old Yellow Garage* 97

Chapter 12 – *Pothole from God* 107

Chapter 13 – *Snow Angels* 119

Chapter 14 – *How Far is Far* 127

Chapter 15 – *Good-Bye* 133

Epilogue 141

Preface

Maps, I like maps, all kinds of maps. I especially like USGS maps the best, an abundance of details on them. Many people don't use maps much anymore, they like their new GPS's now. A phrase I hear all too often is, "You still use maps?" I've been known to sit and pour over the details of a region by studying a map for hours. I even use a magnifying glass to get up close; I don't want to miss anything. There is so much remarkable information on maps. You can go anywhere with them. They can take you to the four corners of the world and everywhere between. You can let your imagination run as you picture your next journey down the road.

I studied surveying in college where I learned how to collect information and then draw a detailed map to scale – got an A+. Fascinating class, right up my alley, enjoyed every aspect of that course. Maps, unlike GPS's show you the big picture, and in color too! Yes, I know GPS has color but maps give greater detail and terrain features. You have altitude, contour lines, direction, coordinates, city and park details, mileage charts, distances between points, exits, rivers, lakes, streams, picnic areas, trails, beaches, golf courses, and most importantly, all the roads you need to get where you are going. You have all that information at your fingertips, all in one easy to read book.

How many have a driver's license? Please raise your hand. How long have you been driving? Me, I earned my driver's license back in high school, probably, like you did. I remember sitting in the backseat, as a young pup watching my father drive the old family station wagon. It looked so complicated at the time. There were so many buttons to push, handles to turn, pedals to push, and the steering wheel – forget about it! I was impressed. It came to pass that I, too, would learn how to push those buttons, turn the handles, push pedals, and steer a car.

How did you get to drive? You read the manual, took a driver's Ed course in high school, and then you took the "test." That test will prove to the instructor, parents, and friends alike, you are entitled to move from the backseat to the front driver's seat. You move more slowly at first taking care not to get a ticket or get in an accident. There are other drivers out there doing the same thing – "If they can do it, so can I," you tell yourself.

God, you will remember, gave old Moses some important directions for mankind to follow. There were only ten directions to get you where you needed to be. The Bible is full of stories of generations of people, young and old, steering off the road of life into a ditch. Today, if you get into trouble on the road, there is always "Roadside Assistance" to help pull you out of that ditch.

As you read through these true stories, hopefully, you will find a lesson in each one. Some of these episodes go back several years, some fairly recently. At the time, I failed to see what the Good Lord was attempting to demonstrate to me. I look back and say, "Oh, now I get it." As I was thinking about putting these events into this book, I prayed and asked God to help me. He answered my prayer and told me, "You write the stories, as they happened, and I'll do the rest." He hasn't disappointed me. At the end of each story, you will find my version of 'Roadside

Assistance;" this is the section where you can search for the significance of the story, in your life, and what lesson is in there for you. Everyone will have a different meaning and a different conclusion.

Everyone has a story to tell. Moses, Christopher Columbus and Lewis and Clark did not have maps, but they did carry another Book with them on their journey, God's Book. God is looking for you on the road He is on and hoping you are going His way.

You are about to embark on God's road trip through the eyes of this Road Warrior, enjoy your journey.

Acknowledgements

Unless you committed your life to living as a hermit, God intended us to live together, side by side with each other. Such is the case in writing a book like this one. It cannot be accomplished alone. Many others were involved in this process.

There are many thanks to those people, in these stories, who I will never meet and whose names I will never know but crossed my path. They had no idea what impact they would have in my life and, hopefully, in yours after you are finished reading. Their actions had a purpose and created events that God intended.

Many thanks to those personally responsible for helping me during this project. Thanks to Dave Barnhart for his timeless effort in helping through the editing portion, and for his fantastic friendship these past several years. Many thanks to Sam Frey for his incredible friendship and guidance. I would not be where I am today without these two Godly men in my life.

Thanks to Andy Sanders at 5 Fold Media for connecting me with my publisher, Dean Drawbaugh. Thanks to Dean who has the professional wisdom to take on my book and walk me through it all and for his patience in dealing with me.

Many thanks to my wife, Sherry, who without her guidance and wisdom, I would not have even started this book. She encouraged me to see these stories through God's perspective. She guided, nourished, and supported me when I needed it the most.

I do thank God for His unconditional love and for pulling me close to Him in good times and bad.

Chapter 1

"Junk-Drawer"

"What lies behind us and what lies before us are nothing compared to what lies within us."

Ralph Waldo Emerson

Go to your kitchen, garage, office, workshop, glove compartment or any place a simple drawer can collect junk. If you are like most, it's a mess. Everyone has a messy junk drawer someplace in their life. If you were to go to my kitchen, you would find the top drawer to the right loaded with odds and ends from years of collecting. Most of the items are worthless, but way down in the bottom you would find a few pieces of unforgotten, but valuable memorabilia. Every once in a while, we get that "urge" to clean out that drawer and sort out all that stuff. Most of it goes in the garbage. The rest gets shuffled around and organized into places in the drawer for future cleanings. "Sure," we say, "I'll use this someday," and fail to file it in the file cabinet under the sink. When we have finished our task with the cleaning it looks neat and organized, for about a minute. But within weeks, or often, days, it's a junk drawer again. Useless pieces of string, old rubber bands, broken pencils, thumbtacks, and such fill the drawer to the overflowing point once again.

Some companies even cash in on our inability to keep our lives neat and organized. They market little drawer keepers to help keep our junk away from other junk. Much like those special dinner plates with little dividers that keep food away from other food, some people don't want their junk touching other pieces of junk. They work for a while but when overloaded, those little compartments seem to fade out of sight until the next bout of "clean it up and throw it out" hits us. Somebody is making a lot of money on our junk. But, do not despair, whenever we are looking for that piece of string or loose thumbtack, we know exactly where to run first.

The usual cleaning takes place after we tried to fix the broken whatever. And for the last three months we couldn't find the little tube of crazy glue. But after looking for an old rubber band in our workshop drawer, we came across the glue. It's all connected.

You know it's in there, and you pull the drawer out too fast and too far and you find yourself on the floor scooping all the contents into your hands and back into the drawer. Right then and there you vow to clean out and organize that junk drawer.

Most vehicles are no different. Everyone has a glove compartment. When was the last time you kept a pair of gloves in there? They rarely get cleaned out. Mine – it's full. Now, newer cars and even worse, pickup trucks have even larger storage bins to hold more junk. They installed these larger compartments between the front seats to act as a catch-all for the everyday junk that seems to gather unnoticed. They have little compartments all over the vehicles now, in the doors, front and back, under the seats, along the sides of the hatchback, under the hatchback, they're everywhere, and they're all full! I even installed a truck box in the bed of my pickup truck, and it's full. In there, you will find maps for many of the Northeast states, ratchet straps for holding down that piece of wood I need, rags, chains, rope and much, much more.

Let's take this junk-drawer idea a couple of steps up the ladder. Our minds have all stored away, in the back, some little left-over story or some little incident that made us laugh or even cry at times. Over time, these stories build up and start taking over the space designed for far more important issues like birthdays, anniversaries or meetings we're not supposed to be missing. We try our level best to organize these thoughts and clean them up and throw them out. Most stories are kept. They are stored way in the back somewhere. We can't throw away old memories too quickly. But unlike the junk drawer in our kitchen or vehicle, we need most of them and want to hold onto them. We need them around as reminders of when or who made us laugh.

These stories are part of my personal "junk-drawer." It's the stuff of over forty years that has survived the "clean-it-up-and-throw-it-out" syndrome that often seizes me from time to time. We have our personal junk-drawer. We seldom sit down and take the time to record these thoughts or stories on paper for fear of being laughed at. It has taken me several years to get to the point of opening my own drawer.

Some bad memories that I have been trying to throw out for years would automatically resurface, but regardless, they're in there with the good ones. Traveling along the roads of this great country has produced many of these memories.

As with the cleaning out of any junk-drawer we usually start with the larger items and work our way down to the bits and pieces. As we work through the process, we find ourselves with all those little pieces way in the back.

These stories will follow much the same process. I will start with the bigger stories and end with these little stories toward the end. Without failing, I will find something at the bottom of all that junk, and it will remind me of another "Road Warrior" story. It will find its way into the middle somewhere. It might not fit there exactly, but most junk doesn't fit anyway.

There is no rhyme or reason for any particular way this will be put together. It will just happen as I clean out. All of these stories are recollections of what happened while traveling along the roads of America. They are all true.

I hope and pray you get out of them what I have gleaned from them through the years. One last thing, go to your car or truck. Open your glove compartment – it's in there; the junk-drawer of our mobile life. Those that have trunks – beware!

Roadside Assistance

"The cave you fear to enter holds the treasure you seek."
Joseph Campbell

Maybe you've walked up to your spiritual junk drawer, peeked in and closed it quickly in fear of letting something out. "What will others think?" I came across a story; year's back, about the game of Hide-and-Seek and how adults play this game. We want to hide, we want to be sought out, but truly confused about being found. "I don't want anybody to see." God already sees.

The time it takes to clean out your "Junk Drawer" can vary. Many are afraid to do the clean up and throw it out routine. Many are afraid of what they might find. The physical junk drawers in our lives differ much from the mental or spiritual junk drawers. This apprehension keeps us always on the edge of knowing;

"What's in there?" Better still is, "Do I want to deal with it?" Many don't.

Some of these stories, taken out of my personal junk drawer, have been in there for over forty years. How much junk do you have in your Junk Drawer? Have you been able to open and peek inside? Can you open it? Does fear stop you from going any further? What will you do when you finally have the courage to open it?

God is by your side every step along the way. When time came to start this book, He made a promise to me. "You open the drawer, tell others what's in there and I'll do the rest." We are on this road together, and I'm not the driver this time.

Meditate on:

How much do you deal with or stuff in your Junk Drawer hoping never to see it again or ask God for help in taking the first step?

_____
_____
_____
_____
_____
_____
_____

Pray on:

Ask God to show you how to deal with the junk in your draw and what you can do to take the next step. He already sees the load you are carrying and wants to help you stay on His road.

_____
_____
_____
_____
_____
_____
_____

CHAPTER 2

Another Delay

"Treasured travel suggestions are dancing lessons from God."

Kurt Vonnegut, Jr.

My profession takes me to some of the most exotic destinations. My travels have taken me through Bethlehem, Nineveh, Peru, Rome, Berlin, Athens, Poland, Florence, Dublin and even Paris. Unfortunately, they do not resemble their romantic ancestral cities of old Europe. All these locations exist here in New York, Vermont, New Hampshire and the Northeast. Year to date, October 2013, I have driven the equivalent of circling the globe at the equator, over 24,000 miles. You get to see some amazing sights along the way. Some, well, not so pleasant.

If you want to see some scary sights, spend some time on America's roads. You'll experience people reading a book, putting on make-up or eating a bowl of cereal. And I'm not talking about passengers either, no; I'm talking about drivers! I give them plenty of space as they pass me like I am standing still! I was once behind a guy in his pickup truck. What came next is hard to comprehend. His left arm poked out his window as he dumped his half-full hospital urinal out onto the street! Yes, the kind with a handle you get while in the hospital when you can't make it to the bathroom. It's a portable bedpan for guys. It sprayed all over the place! I could not find a carwash fast enough; I ran it through twice just to make sure!

The worst is the "right on red." If they can fit their Hummer between you, and the car in front of you they will. "*I have no need to stop here, I can fit it in.*" I even had a police officer turn right on red right in front of me without stopping! I guess he had special privileges. I almost hit him. One person commented to me that painted road lines are just suggestions. Remind me to tell you the story when I pulled over a State Trooper, for real, no kidding, true story. His taillight was out, and I hated to pass up the opportunity to tell him so, he took it all in jest and with a smile, but that's another story.

You can experience some beautiful sights along the way as well. Experiencing all four seasons on the road is especially pleasurable. Last week was unique; my travel commitments took me to Vermont and New Hampshire. Between New York and Vermont is beautiful Lake Champlain, a wanna-be "Great Lake." The cities of Plattsburgh and Burlington lie to the north and the historic village of Ticonderoga to the south, complete with the Old Fort Ticonderoga. It's a fine lake 125 miles long, 14 miles wide, and 400' deep. Its claim to fame is "Champ" the equivalent of Loch Ness, hundreds of claimed sightings going back over 200 years.

There are two bridges, one at the uppermost part, on the Canadian border, and one halfway down and hosting several ferries in between. I usually know where I'm heading when navigating between the two states, using my maps, but this particular day I followed my GPS. The "why" will come later. It didn't take me over the newly rebuilt Crown Point Bridge at the lakes' halfway point; it took me to one of "those" ferries. I did not want to hold court, in my head, over what would be the best route. I was there so I might as well save the forty-mile round-trip up over the bridge and down the other side. Upon arriving at the ramp to the ferry, I notice the usual sight – the ferry was pulling away. As "Get Smart" would say; *"I missed it by that much."* Just like the movies they arrive as the ferry is pulling away. I'm not the daredevil type on the road, anymore, and was not about to speed down the ramp and attempt to "jump on." The gate was down; the ramp was up and the ferry was westward bound for Ticonderoga, New York. Being a road warrior, I have learned not to get upset at life's trivial inconveniences. I shut the engine down and resigned myself to watching the ferry pull away. I decided to wait for the return trip, I had little choice; *"Another delay."* But then – then it happened! Could it be? How is this possible? Things like this don't usually happen, at least, not to me. The ferry slowed, stopped, reversed all engines and BACKED UP! I'm not kidding! I sat up to see the first mate raise the gate and wave me on! Totally stunned and amazed, I stumbled to start the engine and drove on. I'm sure the other passengers, on the ferry, were just as befuddled. Amazed and grateful I got out to pay the toll and saw the captain tip his hat. I went over and shook his hand, heck I wanted to give him a hug; instead I gave him a $5 tip and thanked him.

Every once in awhile something or someone surprises you. That little act restored my faith in human nature. The unexpected happened. In a world of *"me, me, me,"* here were a captain and his first mate as they made an executive decision to return to shore and retrieve one more passenger. I stood on the deck of the ferry and enjoyed the beautiful fall foliage up and down both shorelines. I reveled in the glory and blessings of the Almighty. He used this delay to teach a lesson. Delay if we accept it, can produce the quieter virtues – humility, patience, endurance, and persistence. Good qualities are the last to be learned. He looked down upon me that day and dropped a little "candy kiss" in my lap. *"Here, this one's for you; I know how much you needed it today."* People wonder, *"Why do good things happen to bad people?"* But sometimes good things happen to just ordinary people. The sun wasn't shining that autumn day, but it was glowing brightly inside. The balance of the trip home was a blur. I kept looking on my lap at the "candy kiss" from above. And oh, thank God for His GPS. God is never in a hurry, but He is always on time. Enjoy your travels and expect the unexpected.

Roadside Assistance

"If everything comes your way, you are in the wrong lane."
Author Unknown

Driving can take a toll on the driver. It can be fun, and it can be a nightmare. Can you remember an incident where you couldn't figure out how you got out of it? You knew something bad was about to happen and when you looked it had disappeared. How did you react? Can you replay, in your mind, the event over and again? Is it possible God saw it too and was watching? Not all events have a happy ending like mine, but more often than not we experience them and don't even recognize them for what they are, Candy Kisses from heaven. God is by your side and hoping you will call for His help. He is always going your way.

Meditate on:

When God gets involved, the least likely things happen to the unexpected. Each situation God has for you may not always come in the package you expected. But He will always provide you with the love you always need for that situation.

_____
_____
_____
_____
_____

Pray on:

Lord, life is full of surprises, some are beautiful and some are painful. I am incapable of controlling those circumstances, but I can control my attitude. Help me to be present in those moments and embrace the lesson You are trying to teach me through the unexpected. Amen.

_____
_____
_____
_____
_____

Chapter 3

Signs

"Why pay for GPS when Jesus gives directions for free."
Author Unknown

What's a sign? Why do we have them, and why so many? We've all seen them; they're everywhere. Try going through the day without using one or even seeing one. The dictionary defines the word "sign" as: a token, indication, object, action, event, pattern that conveys a meaning. A symbol used as an abbreviation the word or words represent. A notice bearing a name, direction, warning, or advertisement displayed or posted for public view; a store sign, a traffic sign.

A sign tells you something. Whether you like it or not the sign is there, and it has a message to convey. They're there to advertise, warn, help, entice, or simply just to annoy you. You can go back as far as the caveman and there on the walls of their caves are signs. Man throwing a rock or stick at an animal for his dinner, or to impress that "special someone" he'd like to drag back to his cave.

As a road warrior, the most common signs are traffic signs. They are even designed, so you don't need to read them anymore, they just have pictures on them. Sometimes you have to do a double take to make sure you got the desired meaning. There's the red circle with the red diagonal line through a picture telling you "no smoking," "no left turn," or "no U-turn." The list goes on and on; you get my point. I've even seen solar powered 'STOP" signs! The power flashes red warning for you to "STOP" in case you didn't see the big red octagon.

I saw a sign that said "NOTHING FOR THE NEXT 22 MILES." There was nothing there, so someone had to post a sign telling you there was nothing there. Another sign said, "THIS SIGN IS NOT IN USE." Or how about the sign that read, "THIS SIGN HAS SHARP EDGES – DON'T TOUCH THE EDGES-YOU WILL GET CUT." Who thinks of these?

Then there are the crazy signs. Signs put up to help the confused be more confused. "POLICE STATION TOILET STOLEN-COPS HAVE NOTHING TO GO ON." I saw this somewhere; I can't recall where, the sign made me lose all sense of memory and reality. Or the construction sign where three lanes of traffic have been funneled into one lane. The flashing sign reads: "YOU'LL NEVER GET TO WORK ON TIME – HA-HA." First they put up a sign warning you about the traffic jam then they rub it in. But the next sign helps a little; "ROAD CLOSED-YOU ARE EXCUSED FROM WORK TODAY." I'm not sure the boss took that road to work this particular day. Then you have the "HOSPITAL CEILINGS ARE BORING TO LOOK AT-PLEASE SLOW DOWN" sign, or the sign on the winding road, "BE GENTLE ON MY CURVES." And the sign after that one reads, "ACCIDENTS ARE PROHIBITED ON THIS ROAD." I once saw a mattress lying in a ditch; there was a sign next to it: "Rest Stop." One recent sign I saw on the back of a casket delivery truck read: "Don't text and drive; yours may be on the next shipment.

As you navigate these roads, you cannot miss the billboards. These are the biggest signs and cannot be overlooked. Some years back someone invented a three-sided flip around billboard. Every minute it would turn to a different sign. This way one billboard had three separate distinct messages. Now they are electronic, like a colossal TV screen, multiple messages all at once. Someone had paid big money for this one set of billboards. They consisted of a simple black background with a few white words on them. They read, "WHAT PART OF 'NO' DIDN'T YOU UNDERSTAND?" or "WE NEED TO TALK," or, "YOU THINK IT'S HOT NOW?" And my favorite, "DON'T MAKE ME COME DOWN THERE." All these billboards were signed on the bottom right; "GOD." The last one I remember seeing was; "IS THE ROAD YOU'RE ON GOING TO GET YOU TO MY PLACE?" I like that one.

A story is told of a potato farmer. After several years of harvesting potatoes, his farm began to fail, and his expenses exceeded his proceeds. One year his farm yielded little to no potatoes. He walked out into his dry, parched field and fell prostrate on the ground. He bent over and cried to the Almighty, "Lord, help me; I've planted these fields for years, and you have blessed me tremendously, now there is nothing."

He leaned back and with arms stretched skyward, and pleaded with the Almighty, "What do you want me to do?" The clear blue sky showed two distinct clouds forming two letters, "P C." The farmer jumped up and yelled out, "Thank you Lord. I will go out and Preach Christ!" He took his remaining savings and took off to "Preach Christ."

Not long after, he returned home, broke, tired, and worn out. The following morning he returned to that same spot in his field and knelt again prostrate to the Almighty. "Lord, I did what you said. I went out to preach to the world and nothing happened. What do you want me to do?"

Out of nowhere "BOOM!" "THIS IS THE LORD, PC – PLANT CORN!"

The Lord will send signs to those looking. He always sends signs it's how we translate them. We need the power of the Holy Spirit to help translate them. Without the Holy Spirit, we just see signs and not the message. Sometimes we even fail to see the sign.

God has sent many signs through the years. The Bible is full of them, many were heeded, and many more ignored. As time continues to run out during these Last Days, the signs God has sent are staring at us daily. Jesus said, "When it is evening, you say, 'It will be fair-weather, for the sky is red.' "And in the morning, 'there will be a storm today, for the sky is red and threatening.' You know how to see the appearance of the sky, but cannot see the signs of the times? "An evil and adulterous generation seeks after a sign; and a sign will not be given it, except the sign of Jonah." And He left them and went away. Matthew 16: 2-4

"The disciples came to Him privately, saying, "Tell us, when will these things be? And what will be the sign of Your coming, and of the end of the age?" Matthew 24:3

And Jesus answered and said to them: "Take heed that no one deceives you.

For many will come in My name, saying, 'I am the Christ,' and will deceive many. And you will hear of wars and rumors of wars. See that you are not troubled; for all these things must come to pass, but the end is not yet.

For nation will rise against nation, and kingdom against kingdom. And there will be famines, pestilences and earthquakes in various places.

All these are the beginning of sorrows." Matthew 24: 4-8

Many are not interested in paying attention to these signs today. It would mean they would have to change and turn to Him. The signs are there; the signs are everywhere. We just have to see them and act, time is running out. Over the head of Jesus, on the cross, was a sign that read; "THIS IS JESUS, THE KING OF THE JEWS." Pick up your cross and follow me, He says. The billboard sign bears repeating, "IS THE ROAD YOU'RE ON GOING TO GET YOU TO MY PLACE?"

Roadside Assistance

"The shortest distance between two points is under construction."

Noelie Alito

Can you remember a simpler life as a child? Can you recall your world as a more peaceful place? We live in difficult times today. They are not easy anymore. Each day brings worse news than the previous one and with no end in sight.

Signs can be warnings of impending danger or even forthcoming rewards. The signs evident in today's world are clear for all to see. The Bible is absolutely clear on this subject. Many others throughout history have proclaimed they saw the same signs, and the ending of this age was near. These are exciting times to be alive. NEVER have ALL these signs existed in so many places around the globe with such frequency and intensity. We are the first generation to witness ALL the signs mentioned in the Bible. But the scoffers will continue to argue against it.

Satan knows the end is close at hand and continues his siege on humanity. He persists on bringing, into the spotlight, certain people to help perpetuate the lie that he doesn't even exist. Many people confuse the term "end of the world" with "end of the age." They are not the same. The world will continue but not as we know it today. The age of grace is closing quickly, and the new Millennial Kingdom will soon be upon us. With the signs, given in the Bible, we know the end is near. Matthew 24:33, "So likewise ye, when ye shall see all these things, know that it is near, even at the doors." We see ALL these signs coming upon us.

This world is being turned on its head, and we need to be ready. We live in a time like no other in history. If you are not a Christian and believe these signs, please put your trust in Jesus before He brings judgment upon the whole world. A large portion of the population strongly refuses to consider the prospect of prophecy being fulfilled in our generation. In all honesty, many of these people probably have a good reason for not wanting to see the end times: the start of the tribulation would signal their doom.

Can you deny what is occurring right around you? Can you change these circumstances? The only thing you can change is where you will spend eternity. We are all sinners and fall short of the glory of God. Do you believe you are a sinner? Do you want to be forgiven of those sins? There is only one-way, and that is Jesus. "He is the way (the road), the truth and the life…" Are you on the same road?

Meditate on:

The truth is that every human being is born blind to the spiritual things in the Lord Jesus and our eyes and ears need to be opened. People are blind and deaf until God opens their eyes to see and ears to hear. You may very well be an intelligent person, but when it comes to the gospel, there is an unusual capacity not to understand. You may have a Masters in science but fail to understand the simple plan of salvation. This is the strategy of Satan.

Pray on:

Lord, open my eyes and ears for the things I need to learn. Keep me from a life of ignorance that maintains the devil's domination over my life.

Chapter 4

Pulled Over

"Only those who risk going too far can possibly find out how far it is possible to go."
                                                                T S Eliot

Anyone who is old enough to be reading this is old enough to be behind the wheel of a vehicle. Whether it be a motorcycle, car or truck, you can drive. You've been driving, perhaps, since high school. That could be quite a few years for the majority and not so for others. We are drivers that's how we get from place to place, either it be for school, work, soccer moms, scout dads or vacations, we drive.

Not everyone has an occupation like mine where your pickup truck is your office. I drive for a living; I drive a lot. You drive a lot too; I'm sure. Each of us, at one time or another, has seen a police officer, state trooper, or a local sheriff on the road. I am sure there isn't one of you out there that hasn't seen those red and blue, bright flashing lights in your rearview mirror approaching your tail at lightening speeds. Your heart starts pounding; your mouth goes dry; your grip on the steering wheel tightens, and your mind starts running away. "What did I do? I wasn't speeding; he can't be after me!" You slow down and pull over slightly hoping he moves past you. The speeding police car zooms past and pulls in behind the car in front of you and pulls him over. Your pulse slows, and you let out a little chuckle, "Ha, got 'cha that's what you get for speeding!" And you drive off a freeman for another day. You have, probably, driven by an officer who has pulled someone over, same chuckle, "Ha, got 'cha!"

Then there are times when it's your turn, the person pulled over is you. Whether you were speeding or you had a broken taillight, "he got 'cha!" There are stories of women crying their way out of it, or the batting of the eyelashes. Both hope to be released from the little paper with his signature on it requesting your presence at the local courthouse. He's kind during the whole process, but the courthouse party awaits you. We've all been there. Rare is the driver who has not either seen a trooper pulling someone over or been the one pulled over.

In many states across the west, the speed limit has been raised to 70 and in some places, 80 miles per hour. Local troopers have placed, in the median, life-size replicas of trooper cars. From a distance, they look real. On closer inspection one can see, they are painted plywood to imitate a trooper on the prowl. The process helps to slow down the "speeders." In some city locations, they place color vinyl copies of huge potholes in the middle of roads. This act causes drivers to slow down and drive around the fake potholes. They even move them around to confuse the locals after they figured out the scheme.

Most of us don't live in Mayberry, RFD. Sheriff Andy Taylor is not standing outside your car wishing you a great day and to "be careful out there." "Aunt Bea has a hot apple-pie with my name on it, got to go." No, we live in the real world. Troopers are real, and so are the tickets. I drove through Mount Airy, NC once during a road trip. It is the hometown of Andy Griffith. You can feel Mayberry all around you, and you can even eat at Aunt Bea's Diner; I had a Barney Burger. I could have sworn I saw

Deputy Fife in the next booth polishing his single bullet.

I wondered what it would be like to be on the other side of the car door looking in. Well, the Good Lord offered me the opportunity not too long ago. What you are about to read is the story as it unfolded. My memory is not the best these days, but it is clear about that day. You never forget an incident like this.

It was a rural road, country setting; I'm on a two-lane straight road heading down a long hill. Someone freshly painted the dotted yellow line down the middle. There are two vehicles on the road heading in the same direction. I'm in the second vehicle. Yep, you guessed it; the car in front of me was a state trooper, local station. Wondering to myself, "Am I speeding? Are my headlights on? Is my seat belt fastened? I'm not on my cell phone. Why is he slowing down? Uh Oh." Just then he turns on his right blinker. He's making a turn, OK, no problem. The first thing one does after turning on their blinker is to start braking; I notice his left brake light is out. "Ha, got 'cha!" I said to myself out-loud. Here's my golden opportunity. These don't come by too often in a man's life, but here's mine.

Courage or insanity, I'm not sure. I start flashing my high beams at him. "What, are you crazy?" is running rampant around my brain. I don't stop. He makes his turn and slows down to see what I'm going to do. I follow him. He pulls over to the dirt shoulder of the side road. I pull up next to him as he is rolling down his window. There is a cloud of apprehension over his car, and it is pouring out of his window. I could tell his right hand was nowhere in sight, probably on his sidearm ready for action. "I got me a crazy one here!" he says to himself. I rolled down my passenger side window. His eyes have that "what are you doing?" look in them. "Can I help you?" asks the bewildered trooper. "Yes officer," I replied. "I just wanted to let you know that your left brake-tail light is out." He gave me a little smirk like, "You're kidding me, right, you actually pulled me over to tell me that!" I said, "Look, I'm going to let you go with a warning this time. Please get that light fixed; I don't want to have to do this again." There is a long pause from both vehicles. He starts chuckling, looks down, and says, "Yes sir, I'll get that taken care of I can." "You have a nice day," says I and we wave good-bye to each other and go our separate ways. I am smiling in disbelief at what I just did and he, almost certainly, doing the same.

I know I got away with that one, and most troopers are not that polite. The last part of this story is how did the trooper explain this, if he did, to his fellow troopers back at the barracks? Somewhere, somehow, I know there is a trooper laughing and telling the story about the time he was "pulled over."

Roadside Assistance

"The best car safety device is a rearview mirror with a cop in it."

Dudley Moore

Not that I recommend this tactic for anyone reading this, but there are opportunities in your path. There are times when you're standing at a crossroad or a fork in the road, and a decision is at hand. Are you able to discern which path is yours? Can you use prudence as your guide, prudence being, mature deliberation, wise choice and correct action. We face this process multiple times daily. The first two parts are easy; it's that last "correct action" part that often leads us down the wrong road in life. Often our simple shortcuts lead us into major traffic jams.

Getting pulled over by a trooper is the easy part, paying financial retribution for our error is the punishment the court hands out and that part hurts.

I see God as the ultimate trooper. He is keeping a record of all our infractions and is holding all the tickets, and they need to be paid. Do you think you're going to get away without a ticket for something you've done? Have you ever pondered how those tickets are to be paid? Nothing you do goes unnoticed by God; He sees everything you do. He has a dash-cam on you. Sometimes He puts roadblocks in your path to help you see you're on the wrong road, and you need to get back on the correct one. How are you able to recognize which is the correct road? This is where using GPS is helpful – "God's Positioning System."

Meditate on:

We've all experienced moments in our life when we hear ourselves say, "YES" to a situation we know deep in our heart isn't right for us. And still we do it. There's only one-way to live life on your right track. Listen to the Spirit in your heart; it holds the secret to your fulfillment of joy and happiness. You can take wrong turns in life, and they can cause you harm; you can either run or learn from it. When was the last time you slowed down, pulled over and looked into God's window? He happens to be going your way.

Pray on:

Father, I am confident that when I make a mess after taking a wrong turn, You can turn me back to You and help me find my way. Help me to be obedient and willing to listen to you. I want to turn away from doing it my way to doing it Your way. Jesus, You are the way, the truth and the life. Amen.

Chapter 5

The Cardboard Sign Read – Homeless

"Whoever is generous to the poor lends to the Lord, and He will repay him for his deed."

Proverbs 19:12

There is a sign I saw recently, it read, "*HOMELESS – WILL WORK FOR FOOD – THANK YOU – GOD BLESS.*" A young man in tattered, soiled clothes holds up a makeshift cardboard sign. Our eyes connect. Everyone has seen these folks; they're all around, especially in the larger cities. They're on the street corners, in parks, under overpasses, in cardboard boxes. I've have seen them under bushes trying to stay warm and dry, they are the homeless.

Hunger is not something to be taken lightly, never been truly hungry, don't want to be. I rolled down my window and motioned him to cross the one lane of stopped traffic near the mall. I handed him two one-dollar bills. It seems these mega-malls are magnets for the homeless, lots of people with money milling around. My 12-year old son sat silently next to me taking this all in. On his lap is a box of freshly baked apple turnovers we just picked up at the bakery, still warm. They're the kind with the white frosting dripping over the edges. The sweet smell of apples and flaky crust filled the truck cabin, and the anticipation of biting into these crunchy delicacies was overwhelming. The plan was to dive into these delightful munchies during our two-hour road trip north for a weekend of camping in the Adirondacks. Without a word or notice, he rolled down his window and handed his prize box of goodies to the man. He had paid for them with his own money! He smiled at me, and I returned the gesture and we drove off in silence side by side. I was never as proud of him as I was that morning. I could see my "Daddy License" shining as it hung on the wall.

I don't claim to know much about the homeless, never been there, never want to be. Growing up you rarely saw a homeless person. Statistics are for bean counters, but I am sure there is a lot more homelessness today there ever was. It is a problem, and it is getting worse, it is not imagined. The recent economic downturn has produced its share of homeless people, people from all walks of life. Society has not done its job properly; it has succeeded in letting some people down. These people are jobless, homeless and hungry.

Not much time passed after this occasion when one of my co-workers returned from lunch. He was complaining about the homeless on the street corner at the same area mall. I sat quietly and listened to the ongoing conversation forming. Slowly, one by one, other fellow co-workers added their comments and complaints. The fever pitch was rising. Their one major complaint was that some of these "homeless" aren't really homeless. They are successful beggars. They leave their assigned posts at five o'clock, get into their fancy SUV's and drive to their fancy homes in the suburbs. Who knows, maybe some do, maybe, maybe not. Who are we to judge?

To these 'beggars" it's their job, their source of income. But, what about those who are homeless and hungry, do we slight all of them for the sake of a few mistrusting individuals? *"For you have the poor with you always, and whenever you will you may do them good: but me you have not always."* Mark 14:7 I finally stepped into the ongoing conversation. I had hopes of calming some ruffled feathers. I interjected that whenever I see a homeless person I give them a few bucks. "You do what?" asked one. "Don't you know you are only encouraging them? You are part of the problem," yelled another! "You shouldn't be supporting them."

Where have we gone as a people? I was taught to help one another. Jesus is quoted in the Bible, "If you do it for the least of my brothers, you do it for me." Matthew 25:40 I truly believe that. "When you feed the hungry or clothe the naked or give drink to the thirsty, you do it for ME." If one of these needy are less than honest with his fellow mortals let God be his judge, not us. Romans 12:19 – "vengeance is Mine, I will repay," says the Lord. There is plenty enough to worry about without worrying about who is in need and who is not. I pity those who do not need it and ruin it for the others who really do. Let us not judge each other. For the measure by which we judge, so shall we be judged. We judge by what we see on the outside, God judges by what He sees on the inside. "Here buddy, take five dollars today, you look like you could use it."

Roadside Assistance

"God pours His love into our hearts to flow out to others' lives."

Author Unknown

Helping someone is not a sin, not helping is. The Bible is clear about this. There are over 300 verses, in the Bible, dealing with the poor, social justice, and God's deep concern for both. We don't like change; it doesn't come quickly for many. Growth doesn't come easily, and spiritual growth is even harder to get. There is a tendency not to be concerned with what should be done for the poor, but what God's thoughts about it are.

God's message is very simple: *help the needy*. It's not hard to grasp; it's just tough to do. Has there been a time when you were in need of something, anything? Did someone fill that need for you? Have you seen anyone in need? Did you fill that need for them? God is clear about rewards for helping the needy. "He who is generous will be blessed, for he gives some of his food to the poor." Prov. 22:9.

What's your next move the next time someone is in need? Give something without remembering and take without forgetting.

Meditate on:

All of us had help at one time, or another whether we want to admit it or not. We had help in accomplishing who we are and where we wanted to be. We must continue to be kind and considerate to others. Helping others helps pave the road ahead of us.

___

Pray on:

Lord, help me to do all the good I can, by all the means you grant me, in all the ways you allow me, in all the places You bring me, at all the times You permit, to all the people You show me, as long as You are with me. Amen.

CHAPTER 6

Problem or Inconvenience

"Unexpected travel suggestions are dancing lessons from God."

Kurt Vornegut, Jr.

My week started out much like the rest. Tuesday was a typical travel day. The inclimate weather slowed my progress on the road. After clocking over 300 miles, with one meeting behind me and one more ahead of me, I knew there would not be enough daylight to sustain the balance of my trip. My destination was Watertown Building Supply in Watertown, NY. Watertown is not one of those famous places one yearns to travel to; there is nothing extraordinary about Watertown. I spent a week there one day.

I ordinarily get to visit this dealer around midday. Arriving later in the day put me at a disadvantage looking for a hotel that night, a real problem. I know there are several local, respectable hotels where I can lay my head comfortably. Pulling off the highway just before 5:00 I knew it was going to be a long night. I called a local hotel, and they told me they were booked solid. Every other hotel, motel in the area for a 50-mile radius was booked as well. Not what I wanted to hear, not a happy camper! Tired, hungry, and now with a major headache I made a call to Mike, my local customer, in Watertown. After much discussion, I asked him what was going on to book every room in a 50-mile radius. He wasn't sure but would make some inquiries. He made several calls for me. After many tries, he found the local Best Western had an opening. I immediately booked it. Upon arrival, the desk clerk told me there was a cancellation just before Mike made his call to them. I was one "lucky" guy to get a room. Getting in out of the snow, rain, wind, and darkness was a blessing. It was a long day, and I wanted something to eat and a place to rest my head for the night.

I settled down on this cold winter's night. I awoke the next morning to more rain, wind, and overcast skies, a typical winter day in New York's North Country. The room came with a complimentary breakfast which was served in the hotels' dining room. On entering, I was greeted by a flood of army khaki uniforms silently eating breakfast. The atmosphere was solemn and peaceful, and the dining room was filled, I was the only one out of uniform. I inquired, to one of the waitresses, what was going on. She told me there was a "switch-out" of troops at the local base, Fort Drum. Watertown is not famous for much, a little history from the War of 1812, but the big news is Fort Drum. This base is home for the 1st Pioneer Division. The 'switch-out" is a twofold operation. There are hundreds of troops, from around the country returning home from Iraq only to be followed by hundreds of troops being transported back to Iraq. This is their home base.

My heart sank. The night before I was angry and bemoaning about not being able to find a room for the night, a real inconvenience.

Here were hundreds of men and women, young and old in this single dining room. They hadn't slept in a real bed for, probably, over a year. They haven't eaten a decent meal, in a real chair, for about the same time frame, a real problem. I was humbled by the sight of these men and women. It made my "problem" seem insignificant, more of an inconvenience. Problem or inconvenience? On the other side of this were the men and women who were getting ready to leave on their tour. They will not see a real bed, or a real toilet or a decent meal at a real table for another year. The worst part is, to think that some of these men and women might not come home at all, again, very humbling, a real problem.

After I had finished my meager meal of Bran flakes and banana, I went over to each table and shook the hands of each soldier. I told them what it meant to see them and to share a meal with them. The smiles on their faces grew larger as we spoke of God and their safe return home. I thanked them for what they were doing. Sometimes you don't know what you've got until it's gone. Sometimes you know what you've got when you see others who don't have it or about to lose it. Most of the time it is not a real problem, it's an inconvenience. A lump in the oatmeal and a lump in the breast are not the same. Not having a bed and not having a place to sleep are not the same.

Only two defining forces have ever offered to die for you, Jesus Christ and the American GI. One died for your soul, the other for your freedom. Psalm 121:7-8 "The Lord will keep you from all harm—He will watch over your life; the Lord will watch over your coming and going both now and forevermore." I quickly came to realize why I was chosen to get that last room the evening prior. I would have gladly given up that room for one of those men or women, but maybe, just maybe, one of them already gave it up for me, I will never know.

Roadside Assistance

"Change is not made without inconvenience, even from worse to better."

Samuel Johnson

We are a spoiled generation; we have been blessed with much. We have much more than our parents had and greater rewards than our grandparents could have imagined. Still, we complain, the line is too long, it's taking too long and it's getting late, I'm starving, I'm cold, I'm hot, it's raining again, when is it going to rain? This list is quite endless. We find reasons to be discontent.

Our personal happiness is not a matter of always getting what we want that is missing in our lives, but rather being able to recognize our blessings and to be thankful. It also means having patience for what is to come. Each favor bestowed on us is a blessing from God; I call them "Candy Kisses." When I get the green light as I'm approaching an intersection, I say a quick "Thank you." When the amount is $4.11, and I happen to have 11 cents in my pocket, I offer a quick "Thank you." We beg, bargain and coerce God into giving us what we think we need; He already knows what we NEED, and THAT'S what we get.

My blessings far outweigh the inconveniences I have faced through the years. Do you recognize your blessings? Do you see God's hand in your daily lives? There are those who will never be content with what they have nor will they be content with what they would like to have. Adam and Eve had it all, the Garden of Eden, a pleasant beginning. They were not content; they wanted the one, single thing that God said was off-limits, just one thing and life has never been the same. The Devil does not come in a red cape and pointy horns; he comes as everything you ever wished for. We know how the story ends and how God's Glory will make us all content.

Do you want contentment? What steps can you take to recognize your blessings? Can you recall that what you now have was once among the things you only wanted? God grants us Candy Kisses sometimes on earth to give us an idea of the paradise of heaven. Lord, help me to be content.

Meditate on:

Count your blessings; it puts the focus on what you do have and not what is missing. Stop and remind yourself, try to be happy with who you are. Stop, and consider why you want something, is it a need or a want. Learn to enjoy the simple things; things that are free are fantastic. Breathe and smile, others will see your smile and laugh themselves. Answer the phone with a smile, they will hear it. Take the time to appreciate your life, think of all the people you're grateful for and thank them with a hug or time spent with them.

_____

_____

Pray on:

Father, help me prayerfully to apply Your Scriptures and help me learn to be content in any and every situation. A godly contentment will fill my heart with peace in place of an anxious heart. Help me to fix my eyes on You, not others as I pursue holiness. In Jesus' name. Amen.

_____

_____

Chapter 7

Long Night in Loon Lodge

Legend says," When you can't sleep at night, it's because you're awake in someone else's dream."

Author Unknown

SINCE we're on the subject of hotels, I had the opportunity to sleep in one recently. As a "Road Warrior" it is difficult to travel without these public, portable domains. The hotel industry is huge. Countless chains of hotels dot the landscape from coast-to-coast, border to border. I stay at one family owned operation, been a Platinum Member for many years. I get to enjoy some nice perks. For one, I get upgraded regularly to the nicer rooms, at no extra cost; you get rooms when there aren't any left. You receive points just for staying there.

This story is not about this hotel chain. This pendulum swung in the opposite direction on this journey. Many times my treks take me to some out-of-the-way places, really remarkable places too, beautiful locations where one can bond with nature and the environment. Mountains, lakes, streams, and wildlife all play an interesting part of the daily routine, a retreat after a long day behind the windshield.

One particular trip took me to the northern regions of Maine. Business called and the planning stages went into motion. I had been there prior and knew some of the general surroundings. I inquired to my business dealer about where to hold our dinner meeting with his staff. He directed me to a local restaurant and lodge located on beautiful Rangeley Lake. I made my reservations for both dinner and lodging. I've never eaten or stayed there; this was my first time.

I arrived and scouted out the establishment. The lodge built in 1909, is a rustic mountain log cabin. It was built as a family summer camp of a wealthy businessman. Original woodwork, artwork and nature photographs from local artists adorned the log walls. The Great Room had "Old Hickory" furniture in front of a large fieldstone fireplace creating a right-at-home atmosphere.

A large moose head hung silently over the split log mantle. I approached the front desk and told the clerk who I was and what the plans for the evening would be. I told him I had made a prior reservation for dinner and a room. He found me in his reservation book, "All is set for your dinner party, sir."

There are only nine rooms in the lodge, not your typical huge hotel type. I was checked in quickly. When I asked for my room key, I was told, "We don't have room keys, there are no locks." That's the first and one of many "firsts" to follow during this one-night visit. "OK," I said, "where is my room?" "Go upstairs and pick one, you're our only guest for the night." I didn't think much about that statement at the time. I walked up the wide, cedar hand-railed stairs to the second floor. I quickly inspected each of the rooms and found a cozy, king-bed room close to the stairs. Nice room with stone fireplace and vaulted ceilings. "I'll have no problem sleeping here," I said to myself.

Back at the front desk, I told the clerk which room I had chosen. "That's an excellent room. I know you'll be comfortable up there tonight. You won't have to worry about any other guests here tonight; you'll be here alone." "OK, no problem, I like the solitude." He gives me a long stare. He says, "Sir, I don't think you quite understand, you will be here alone tonight. Our whole staff leaves at eight o'clock after we close up the restaurant. You're on your own! You will be here all by yourself tonight. We'll put some food in the fridge for your breakfast in the morning. Make sure you close and lock the front door when you leave." "WHAT, how could that be?" They're just going to leave me here all alone by myself. I remembered Steven King lives in Maine. All sorts of horror stories start replaying themselves. All the old Boy Scout campfire stories quickly come to the surface. "Me, alone in this – this creepy place." In one instant, that beautiful, old, rustic, log cabin lodge was transformed into "The House on The Haunted Hill." "There's no way I'm staying here for the night alone," I said to myself. "Aw, come on, grow up, don't be such a baby. You've been in tougher situations than this," I convinced myself.

The dinner meeting went as planned and all my business was completed with a contract in hand. Smiles and handshakes were plentiful as my guests left for the evening from the restaurant. The moment of truth was approaching rapidly. The staff closed the restaurant and they, too, left. There I was, all alone. I went up to my room, ran through my going-to-bed routine and settled into the overstuffed king bed. The only lights were the emergency exit lights. I didn't need to close the door, who was there to check me out? I fell asleep, only to be awakened by that moose head walking around downstairs. The noises this one-hundred-year-old log cabin would make could wake that moose. Vincent Price had nothing on this place! Sleep escaped me most of the night. I awoke at sunrise, to clanging pipes and cracking logs. I did my wake-up duties and gathered my belongings without wasting a minute. I enjoyed a beautiful winter sunrise over the lake as I ate the breakfast they left in the fridge. I then prepared to leave. As I shut the door behind me, I could swear I saw that old moose wink at me, "Bye, you'll come back now, ya hear!"

Roadside Assistance

"I was awake all-night wondering where the sun goes… then it dawned on me."

Author unknown

I didn't get much sleep that night. The darkness was turned into light as the day dawned. The time is coming when we will have a place of rest and peace. John 14:2 "In My Father's house are many mansions: if it were not so, I would have told you. I go to prepare a place for you. Here Jesus assures us there is a place where there are no troubles. And there's room there for each of us if we believe in Him. John 14:3 "And if I go and prepare a place for you, I will come again, and receive you unto Myself; that where I am, there ye may be also." We've got something to look forward to. We can look beyond those sleepless nights and look ahead to the time when Jesus comes for us. Then He will take us home, to be with Him forever.

Sleepless nights come in all degrees. Is it possible God is trying to get your attention about a concern you're trying to deal with on your own? I believe you're awake for a reason. God works the night shift. Spend less time concerned about your issues and trust He is working it out for you. Do you place your troubles at His feet? Do you trust He is not only able to, but willing to resolve your issues?

Meditate on:

When you can't sleep, instead of counting sheep, talk to the Shepherd. "Can't sleep? Talk to Me" – God.

_____
_____
_____
_____
_____
_____
_____

Pray on:

Father, grant me comforting sleep for the refreshing of my soul and body. Give me the gift of peace and a sense of Your presence in the hours of silence during the nights' darkness. Amen.

_____
_____
_____
_____
_____
_____
_____

Chapter 8

And the sky is not cloudy all-day

"The heavens declare the glory of God; the skies proclaim the work of His hands."

Psalm 19:1

WHAT goes through your mind when you hear "The United States of America?" Many of us picture a stunning, majestic Bald Eagle perched atop a tall Douglas Fir tree, or amber waves of grain. Picture it as it soars through a cloudless blue sky; his wings spread wide floating on air. Some see its 330 million people striving to live out their lives like our parents, grandparents, and great-grandparents did. I'm sure you have your own image in your own mind.

It all started back in 1776 with thirteen colonies covering a mere 360,000 square miles. This country has grown to fifty states covering 3,717,813 square miles, 97.77% landmass and 2.23 % water. There are 12,380 miles of coastline and borders Canada and Mexico. Our highest mountain is Mount McKinley in Alaska at 20,236', and Mount Whitney, in the lower 48 at 14,505'. Our longest river is the Missouri at 2,341 miles, and our largest lake is Lake Michigan with 22,394 square miles.

The primary form of transportation, back in those earlier days, was by horse. The train opened vast areas to the west. The transportation revolution started and between 1810 and 1890 railway mania exploded. In 1830, there were approximately 75 miles of railroad track. By the eve of the Civil War, in 1860, there were 29,000 miles of track, and in 1890, the nation peaked with 164,000 miles.

It wasn't long after that the motorcar came along, and life would never be the same. It all began back in 1769 with a steam engine automobile. The internal combustion engine, we know today, arrived in 1885. Since then, they have been improving it. 1908 introduced the Model T Ford, and to think Henry Ford made $1.00 profit from every car he sold. He sold them by the millions! Transportation would never be the same.

I read somewhere that in 1900, there were only 2000 miles of paved roads in the Unites States. The first road paved was Woodward Avenue in Detroit, Michigan. From what I hear it hasn't been repaved since then. There are 3,980,817 miles of roads in the United States today, 2,605,331 are paved and 1,375,486 unpaved. We take for granted these roads. We don't even think about them until they have to be plowed or repaired. We get in our car, truck, motorcycle or whatever and drive off.

Some of the earliest roads, out West, were paved with Redwood planks. They thought the giant Redwood tree was an unlimited resource and could be used for whatever purpose they needed. The giant lumber companies made a lot of money back then. Today one giant Redwood tree, still standing, is worth more than $10,000,000. They are off-limits to loggers. In the East, the early roads were paved with stones or cobbles. Today; asphalt and concrete is the staple for paving, quick, easy, cheap, and long lasting.

Some of these roads lead to nowhere. You can find old logging roads leading up into the woods that just fade away to nothing. One of my earlier passions was to do just that. I'd find an old logging road and take my motorcycle as far back as it would go. There were times I had to drag the back end around facing the opposite direction just to get out of the woods! Roads can take us to work, on vacation, or just a Sunday drive to see what's out there. There are roads, and they need to take us somewhere.

Then you have the cost. These roads are expensive to build. The most expensive highway, to date is the Connecticut Turnpike costing $3,449,000 per mile to build. The Jersey Turnpike was next at $2,200,000 per mile, and the NYS Thruway was $1,547,000 per mile. One seldom thinks of these things while behind the wheel heading off to nowhere land.

As we head down the road, we can take a larger look at these "States." We will see 50 different little "countries" in one. You can be in one state one minute, cross the border into another state and see a totally different environment. Each state is unique in their culture, geography, and people. If, I were to close my eyes and taken to another state I could tell you where we were just by the scenery. The mountains are different; the plains are different, the farms and cities are all different. Each holds their own little gem they call their own.

One of my "Bucket List" goals is to visit all 50 states, I only need 4 more; North Dakota, Louisiana,

New Mexico, and Arizona. My travels have taken me to the four outside corners of the US, San Ysidro, CA; Blaine, WA; Madawaska, ME; and Key West, FL. There is a spot called Four Corners Monument; it's the point where Colorado, Utah, Arizona, and New Mexico all meet. It's the only place in the US where four states touch. Never been there, but if I did go, I can cross two more states off my bucket list.

During an earlier time in my life I had the opportunity, time, and finances to drive cross-country. I got to see some amazing places. This one particular sojourn took me through Oklahoma. It was just after the bombing in Oklahoma City and I chose to visit to see for myself. The original building was demolished, and a chain-link fence encompassed the area and was laden with pictures, prayers, stuffed bears and the like. It was an eerie site and feeling to stand where someone exploded a bomb, killing 168 people, back on April 19, 1995.

From there I drove a few miles to Shawnee, Oklahoma to visit the Fairview Cemetery. Why a cemetery? There you will find a small container at the front entrance. In it are directions to a tombstone, "Here lays Dr. Brewster M. Higley, born in Rutland, OH on November 30, 1823." He studied medicine and became an Otolaryngologist, known as an Ear, Nose and Throat doctor. He lost several wives to injury and disease. The old west was not a healthy place, at times. In a desperate attempt to find a wife and mother for his three young children he married again. This was a disaster. He later left his wife and three children and secretly moved to Smith County, Kansas. There he met and married Sarah Clemons in March, 1875. He spent much of his time writing poems. There along the banks of Beaver Creek, Dr. Higley built a cabin for himself and Sarah. One night he, and his fiddler friend Dan Kelly, with the Harlan Brothers, put one of his poems to music. If you could be transported back to 1871 in a little cabin in Athol, KS, you would hear the debut of "Home on the Range." Yes, Dr. Brewster M. Higley wrote "My Western Home" later changing the title to "Home on the Range."

From there my next stop was Athol, KS. His cabin is privately owned by the Ellen Rust Family. A granite stone, outside the little cabin, bears the original words;

Oh, give me a home where the buffalo roam,
Where the deer and the antelope play, "

Where never is heard a discouraging word
And the sky is not cloudy all day.

You can't recite those words without the tune playing in your head, I can't. The one room cabin stands as a reminder of a time, before we knew, that was hard and also simple. Americans fell in love with the simple song and many added verses of their own as well as the chorus. The song became an icon of the American West and in 1947 "*Home on the Range*" was named the official state song of Kansas.

Where does one travel from here to see more of these states? Well, if you are in Smith County, Kansas all you need to do is head west for 21 more miles on U.S. Route 281. You turn north onto K-191, and travel 1.74 miles. There, just north of Lebanon, Kansas, out in the middle of a privately owned cornfield, is the geographical center of the United States. How they figured this out is way over my head. It was explained that if you cut out the lower 48 states it would balance on a 3" diameter pipe. This pipe stands atop of a 10' tall stone monument. Here, at this spot, Engineers Paulette & Wilson and Surveyor L. A Beardslee calculated it to be.

There is a picnic ground for all to enjoy a leisurely lunch. And not far from there is a small chapel for visitors. One can sit at the center of the United States and ponder the majesty of our God who created this wonderful land. There, you can sit, in the middle of this cornfield and see for 360 degrees. You can watch the clear blue sky and know the heavens declare the glory of God; the skies proclaim the work of his hands. As I drove toward the setting sun, I could hear Dr. Brewster M. Higley, Dan Kelly, and the Harlan Brothers singing their new melody; *"...And the sky is not cloudy all day."*

Roadside Assistance

"All of creation testifies to the power and presence of God."

Margaret Feinberg

Remember the first time you saw a sunset? You gazed up at the sky and saw the sun setting, all the beautiful colors changing constantly. You stood there breathless at what unfolded before your eyes, this splendid painting that changes every few seconds. We see light as it reflects off an object in a certain color, thousands of colors are possible. Light in heaven comes from within and appears to be living; a million-billion colors are possible. As you stand there, you can hear the crickets chirp all around, yet, there are none to be found. You close your eyes and feel transported to a different world. As beautiful, as awe-inspiring as this encounter may be, this is nothing to what it must be like in God's home.

Have you sat by a waterfall as the immense volume of water cascades over the falls? You stand there breathless at this beautiful sight. There are beautiful rivers and waterfalls in Heaven. The water is the purest water, and it dazzles with transparency and life. These are the Living Waters mentioned in the Bible.

Have you taken a walk in the woods in springtime? You see all the beautiful trees and flowers. You look up and feel a gentle breeze coursing through the trees causing the leaves to shiver.

Have you taken a trip to the ocean? Do you remember the first time you saw the ocean? How vast, how immense, how powerful the ocean was as it crashed up against the shore. Your feet shook as the waves crashed on the rocks. You stood there almost out of your senses with delight and thrill at what you experienced. I know people who had God answer their prayers while standing on the shore of the ocean, people who never believed in God before.

As overwhelming, as overpowering as that experience may be, that is nothing compared to what it must be like in God's home in heaven. And you sense the spirit of God's presence all around you and it fills your soul with peace and joy you realize that even that is nothing compared to what it must be like in heaven.

As you travel through these unforgettable experiences you sense, deep down, there is something bigger than you, someone looking down on you. This road, this path, call it whatever you like, you are not alone. What do you feel deep down, as your spine tingles with delight, at these types of memories? Can you shrug them off as if it's just another day, another experience and move on? God's road is narrow and He is your guardrail, ask Him to lend a helping hand to keep you in the center of the road.

Meditate on:

God's goodness is the point of His creation. He colored the world for our delight. God, the engineer of all creation spoke the word and beauty began.

_____
_____
_____
_____
_____
_____
_____

Pray on:

May God, in his good time, reveal His glory in the culmination of his kingdom, where "the righteous will shine like the sun in the glory of their Father." Let those with ears to hear, listen! AMEN.

_____
_____
_____
_____
_____
_____
_____

Chapter 9

Grateful

*"We should certainly count our blessings,
but we should also make our blessings count."*
                                    Neal A. Maxwell

THE open road has been my lifeblood for many years of my professional career. When people ask what I do, I say, "I drive." The real job takes place between those driving episodes. There are, on occasions, where I do not drive – I fly. I still end up driving to the airport; but, the actual distance I travel I do is in the air. As time continues to pass I spend less and less time in the air. I used to like flying. The first time I ever flew, I landed ten minutes before the plane did. I'll fill you in later on the details. Flying has become a real nightmare lately. I'm sure I'm not the only one in this corner. Many claim, since that fateful day back in 2001 that airports are to be feared or at least the airplanes are. If you haven't been on a plane in the past several years, you're missing the experience. Many still enjoy the experience; I'm not one of them.

It wasn't long after that terrible day when the two World Trade Towers were felled that I was to travel to Missouri. I went to help train a new colleague. I drove to Albany International Airport and boarded my plane for St. Louis. It amazed me, years ago; they renamed Albany Regional Airport to the new "International" version. I learned there was one flight going to the Bahamas; and that constituted the new "International" title. I guess it gives them special privileges in the airport category. After arriving in St. Louis, I met my newly appointed counterpart and we were off. He did the driving. I was relieved that I could sit as a passenger and admire some scenery. What a pleasure to be chauffeured!

The week went well, and it was time to return home to upstate New York. I was shuttled to the airport by my co-worker. Before that we stopped at a local winery. The region was famous for its local vintages. This one shop was notorious for its unique and specialty gifts. We stopped and checked it out. There, on the shelf, was a simple tall, crystal wine carafe and four long stemmed crystal wineglasses. Its claim was to have been hand painted with grapes and vines by a local artist, eloquent I thought. I bought it as a gift for someone I knew who would appreciate it. I asked the clerk if she had a roll of clear, wide packing tape. I was going to make a handle and carry it on the plane ride home. Even the box looked hand-painted with a picture of its contents.

My final stop, the airport. I checked my green carry-on bag onto Albany. I wanted to lessen the load of carrying my newly purchased wine carafe and glass set in a box. Security was new with all the highly tightened protocol. TSA, as we know it today, had not yet been born; but, there were security guards checking every bag and box. I gingerly laid the wine box on the moving conveyor belt to be X-rayed. I was careful not to break anything. No problem, all went well, and I was on my way home.

I had a short lay-over in Detroit, which is a pleasant airport, but not so nice people. I arrived early at the gate and was prepared to board for my final leg to Albany, New York. They called my flight, and the door was opened by the agent for boarding. Here is where we take a turn in this saga. This large security woman shows up and stands behind this long table just to the right of the boarding door. I am first in line to board. She gives me the "look!" And with her blue rubber-gloved large index finger, pulled close to her face, starts the wiggling "Come here mister, and come here NOW!" She points that same finger down to the table at the spot where my belongings are to be placed. "This is not going to be a good experience," I'm saying to myself. She grabs hold of the wine set box. She picks it up and starts violently shaking it while holding it next to her ear! I say, "Take it easy with that, its glass." I'm getting that "glare stare." She proceeds to rip it open! I loudly claim, "What are you doing?" "It's already been through security in St. Louis. They x-rayed it and found it to be safe." She doesn't care. She loudly proclaims, "Stand back from the table." She tears it open with no regard to the contents. She pulls everything out, examines it, and shoves it all back in the box. I'm ready to jump the table and wrap that cardboard box around her neck! I say in my best controlled voice, "Do you have any tape to put it back together again?" "NO, that's your problem," says she. "No it's not, why are you doing that to my box?" Now I'm mad. The boarding agent hears the commotion and walks over and says, "Pull him off the flight!" I turned on my heels and loudly exclaimed back "No you're not!" I said. "You're not taking me off this flight because I disagree with your poor handling of an innocent box of glass that security has already checked out and found to be safe. You have no right!" She turned and went back to her door as she waved me off like, "You're dismissed." Strike one!

Everyone that was behind me is now on the plane and in their seats. I, on the other hand, am trying to put my belongings back together, find my place and settle down. It's a short flight to Albany. The plane is expected to arrive around 9:00 PM. I'm a window seat flyer. I'm staring out the window the whole way – not a happy camper. The steam is fogging up the windows; I'm surprised the pilots could see! We are airborne, and the pilot comes on the intercom, "Ladies and gentlemen, we have bad weather in Albany and will take a shot at landing." The landing gear is down; I can see the wet, glossy ground rising quickly to meet the wheels and "Va-room" the pilot hits the throttle, and we are up, up and away! Every eye on the plane turns and stares at me, like I had something to do with this. The pilot comes on and says, "Folks we have severe wind shear and will try to land one more time." He circles the airport and repeats the same routine with the same exact results. You could sense the heightened tension in that plane. He comes on and says the storm is too bad here folks, and we will fly to Syracuse. We will land there and take another flight back after the storm passes. Add this to the day, strike two!

We land in Syracuse and are told, "If you are returning to Albany, stay in your seats, and we will be airborne shortly. If you want to travel back to Albany by bus or have another flight please deplane now." Most deplane and a few remain in our seats. The pilot comes partly down the aisle and is chatting with the flight staff. Me, I'm looking out the window and the crew doing their airport duties down below. The fog has cleared. What do I see? My little green wheelie bag being rolled down the baggage conveyor belt! "Why are they doing this?" say I. Next thing I see is the baggage handler turning around to stack bags on his cart, and MY bag hits the tarmac – BANG! It breaks open, and all my dirty laundry from the week is now on the wet tarmac. He scoops it up and tries his best to put it back. He can't because the zipper is now broken. "That rips it!" I yell. "I have had it, get me off this plane. You told us we were to fly back to Albany, and now you're taking the entire luggage off the plane?" The pilot says, "Oh, we're not flying back tonight." Strike three!

I get off the plane, and I go to the back door where they placed everyone's baggage. I grab my broken zippered, clothes hanging out, green wheelie bag. I have a torn open crystal wine carafe and glass set shredded box under one arm. The broken zipper wheelie bag is tucked under the other arm. I feel like a refugee just off the boat on Ellis Island. It's now 11:30 PM. All the airport shops are closed and no way back to Albany. There is no place to buy a new bag either. A kind woman is closing her store and pulling down the metal security gate. She turns and sees this miserable looking, depressed, tired, hungry man walking past. She says, "Are you OK? Do you need help?" "Yes," I replied. "Come in and let's see what we can do for you." She handed me a half used roll of Duct tape. That was the greatest gift I could have been given, better than a hot meal! I taped up my shredded and torn wine box, and I put a new tape handle on it to carry. I taped up my green wheelie bag the best I could. I gave her a few bucks for her kindness and dragged my tired butt out the door. I was grumbling, all the way, "I will NEVER, EVER fly again."

I recalled that my other counterpart was to be in Syracuse that day working. I called him on my cell phone. He said he was just outside Albany heading for home. He turned around and headed back to Syracuse and picked me up. The rest of the night was a blur. I could not recall much after that. My system totally shut down.

The true story is told about two sisters that were in a concentration camp in Germany during World War II. They were accused of hiding Jews and were taken to one of the camps. One sister managed to sneak a Bible in with her – against regulations, for sure. The conditions there were deplorable. They were overcrowded, and it stunk unbelievably. The food was horrible, and the fleas had overtaken the barracks. They could not believe they could manage much longer under these conditions. This one morning, as they read their Bible in the back corner, they read 1 Thessalonians 5:18, *"Give thanksgiving in all circumstances."*

One sister complained, "I cannot give thanks in these conditions." Her sister told her, "We are together; they could have separated us." "OK, I'll give you that one." "We snuck a Bible in." "OK, I'll give you that one too." "Because it is so crowded nobody hears us reading the Bible in the back corner." "OK, OK, I'll give you that one too. But these fleas! How can you be thankful for these fleas? I am not thanking God for these fleas." Her sister replied, "Be thankful in all things." She explained that they had more freedom in their barracks than the others. The guards would not come in the barracks and would leave them alone to do their thing. Why? The fleas! Thanksgiving changes our perspective.

I failed to see God's glory that eventful flight day years ago. After I had settled into bed upon arriving home, I began my nightly prayers. "Now I lay me down to sleep, having eaten and not been eaten, I thank you Lord for what went right." "For what went right!" I started to think of all the days' events and what went right. The list was endless. I was grateful I had a job. Grateful I had two arms to carry my shredded, torn wine box and my broken luggage. Grateful I could afford to buy a wine gift set. I was grateful I had two legs to walk through the airport. I was grateful I had two eyes to see where I was walking. I was grateful the plane didn't run out of fuel. Grateful the pilots didn't fall asleep while flying. Grateful we didn't get a flat tire upon landing. I was grateful for a million things that went right that day. The list is endless.

Ingratitude will keep us locked up, and gratitude will set us free. It wasn't long before I fell asleep. I slept with an attitude of gratitude in the blessings the Good Lord blessed me with; the good far outweighed the bad. We are to praise the Lord and to thank Him. Strike three? No, it's a new inning.

Oh yeah, the part about landing ten minutes before the plane did. It's true. I went skydiving back in 1972. I jumped out of the plane and landed ten minutes before the plane did. Security didn't even try to stop me!

Roadside Assistance

"The root of joy is gratefulness."

David Steindl-Rast

God gave each of us 86,400 seconds every day. That time can be spent in so many different ways. If we were to look back on that time how can we account for it? Most people sleep 28,800 seconds a night, some more, some less. That leaves 57,600 seconds left for the other things that take up our lives. Between commuting to and from work, working, eating at work that chews up another 21,600 seconds leaving a balance of 36,000 seconds. In our typical time frame that's six hours. That is six hours for each day, 42 hours each week or 2190 hours each year. Have you used one of those seconds to say, "God, Thank You?"

We often pray for a solution to a particular situation in our life, but forget to say "Thank you." Can you remember the last time you stopped what you were doing, cleared your mind and gave God a simple "Thank you?" You can probably remember when you asked, but failed to recall the gratitude. More important are the thank you's for the events that didn't happen that should have. Remember the guardian angel who called as you were walking out the door causing that near miss on the road? Or as you stand on a long line at the grocery store and the clerk calls you over and says, "I'll take you over here."

How did you feel when something went right totally unexpectedly? Many people call that "Luck." With God, there is no luck. "He causes all things to occur for His glory." Are you looking for His hand in your routine? Are you expecting God to show up with His hand on your shoulder, either holding you back or prompting you ahead? He is busy watching out and guiding your every step. Do you let Him know?

When you plant your head on your pillow at the end of each day, say a simple prayer. As you shut down your daily engine pray a prayer of gratitude. Let Him help you overcome evil as you welcome God's hand in yours as He says, "Are you going my way, take my hand?"

Meditate on:

Gratefulness allows you to celebrate the present, helps block envy, resentment, regret, and depression. Grateful people live more stress-free lives and increases self-worth. Even small hearts can hold a large amount of gratitude.

Pray on:

Dear God, thank you for the gifts you have blessed me with, both physical and spiritual. Every day brings new miracles and gifts I would have never seen before, I welcome more tomorrow. I am truly blessed. Amen.

Chapter 10

Outside Rider on an Inside Road

"If you dare nothing, then when the day is over, nothing is all you will have gained."

Neil Garman

THE sign on the wall read, "NO BEER CAN COLLECTIONS ALLOWED IN DORM ROOMS." This sign is placed next to a myriad of other warnings placed there by the college administration in our dorm lounge. They're there for your protection; I was assured. Ok, Ok, OK, I get it; I'm supposed to pay attention and be safe. First, no one reads these signs and worse, no one heeds their warnings. We're in college, and we're not supposed to conform, we're free spirits and invincible.

Me, I'm the king of nonconformity. If everyone liked something, I made sure I didn't. I wanted to be different, and I was. Two of my buddies had amassed a serious beer can collection up in the rafters of their dorm room. The Dean of Students' job was to police these "man caves" to assure their conformity to the rules. First visit, "Guys, these have to go; you know the rules." The usual reply followed, "OK, Ok, we'll do it." Second visit, "Guys, these have to go; I don't want to tell you again." Same reply, "OK, OK, we'll do it." Third visit, "Guys, I told you," and he held up a yard stick and walked the perimeter of the room taking every can to the hard, cold floor and left.

What do you do with 258 empty beer cans? Before taking them to the garbage heap, you have to make something useful out of them. We tried. We made towers out of them. We made columns eight feet tall then walked through them for fun. When that novelty wore off, we had to expand our horizons.

I was the only student on campus with a motorcycle. Not an Evel Knievel by any means but I was in college, remember invincible? Who didn't do something brainless in college? My proposal was to relocate the beer cans to the parking lot behind the dorm. We would erect a beer can pyramid wall as tall as we could. I would then drive my bike through the wall creating a smashing extravaganza. We had one problem not seen by the ever growing crowd – the wind. The college was located on the shores of Lower Saint Regis Lake in upstate New York. Failure was not an option here.

Our dorm measured ninety yards from end to end and had two stories. It had three doors, one at each end and one dead center. I instructed the pit crew to place the beer can pyramid wall in the hallway ten feet before the center door leading out to the parking lot. I drove my bike to the front entrance, and three of us carried it up the stairs into the hallway. I strapped on my helmet; I wasn't stupid – just crazy! The sound of a motorcycle in a confined six-foot wall space is surprisingly thunderous. There, halfway down the hall was the beer can wall, and beyond the wall was the crowd all waiting in anticipation. "Can he do it? Will he do it?" I dropped into first gear. I throttled up and popped the clutch. Down the hall, I flew. Beer cans flew in every direction. The bike stopped right at the door, as planned. It was back in the parking lot in 2.5 seconds, great pit crew. Yes, I was the king of motorcycle daredevil.

The following semester someone wrote an article for the school paper titled, "Dangers in the Dorm."

There, in the article, were the usual hazards. You had your Frisbee Golf in the hallways. You had your mattress bulldog fights. You had broom beer can hockey. But it was the last sentence that has always stuck with me, "But motorcycles in the dorm?" No other word mentioned of who, what, where, when, how and the why!

Looking back on that daredevil day, I can see what I did, but not why. No one challenged me or dared me. If I had been caught, I would have never graduated; I would have humiliated my father and worse, myself. Angels were on overtime that day, and God spared me the humiliation of a disaster. Not a good road to travel but grace was in abundance. I went on to graduate, and that story lives only as a memory of, when I took a different road.

Roadside Assistance

"He knows he's going to die eventually, but he's got a lot to do before he gets there."

Greg Rucka

Being a daredevil does not require many brain cells, just some courage. You can do anything if you're not afraid, and there are critical issues to deal with, we are entitled to our options. There is a fine line between bravery and idiocy and you best know where it lies. I would not go back and replay that event, but I was glad I did it. The dorm hall will never be the same. Thousands of students and parents, alike, have walked that hall and will never know its history.

We travel different kinds of roads during our time here on earth. Has there been a time when you backed down in an individual situation for fear? Can you recall an event that you did something out of the ordinary, and you felt exhilarated because of it? I'm not condoning brain-dead stunts here – just a little glory to hang your hat on. Does watching another daredevil start the adrenaline rushing as you say? "I can do that."

As you journey down this road, you will find many tempting parking spaces. How do you stay on the road and out of these dangerous temptations? Many say they can do it on their own without any help, and fall to these same temptations. God is your Road Atlas keeping you aware of these enticements. What do you do when you realize you parked in the wrong space?

Meditate on:

Courage does not mean fearlessness. Courage is knowing the risk, and possibly even being afraid but having the strength to overcome it. Courage can come in many different forms. Standing up against the evils in this world takes courage.

_____
_____
_____
_____
_____

Pray on:

Lord, I am choosing to lean on you, for when I am at my weakest, Your strength is the strongest. I pour out my grief to You and on that glorious day Your love will conquer all and we shall walk together again down Your road.

_____
_____
_____
_____
_____

Chapter 11

The Old Yellow Garage

Why kindness works:
—Kindness has pure intentions
—Kindness is given freely
—Kindness leaves a lasting legacy

Ron Cooper

THREE hundred miles. Doesn't sound too bad. That's the distance from my front door to my college dorm. You can walk it in fifteen days or bicycle it in six. Driving in a car takes five hours and on my motorcycle eight hours. I graduated from college and decided a visit, to some buddies still on campus, was in order. I was working at the time, in Jersey, and my boss pleaded with me to be back at work first thing Monday morning. I promised I would.

The eight-hour trip up north went well. Had a great time with my buddies and time came for the return trip home. Sunday morning I awoke to cold wind and rain. It wasn't just wind and rain; it was WIND and RAIN! I decided to get as early a start as possible. This road trip was going to be one for the books. I donned my two-piece raingear and helmet and headed south. Fifty miles behind me and two hundred and fifty miles still ahead it hit! "Putt-putt" goes my motorcycle. It died; it just stopped working. Everything shut down. Nada, zip, zilch, ka-put! Bad timing. Having a working knowledge of its parts, I looked at the only fuse it contained. There under the seat is the fuse box with a blown fuse, the little glass kind with the two silver ends. I carried extras for such emergencies and replaced it. "POW" – it blew the moment I turned the key. Not good. I put my last fuse in – "POW," same thing. Now I'm in trouble. The hard rain continues its onslaught assisted by the cold driving wind.

A small RV pulls over, and a sympathetic older gentleman emerges. "Everything OK?" he asks. "No, not really," I replied. "Where are you headed?" "Northern Jersey," I mumbled. "I might have my motorcycle racks with me. I can give you and your bike a ride down; I'm going your way." The clouds parted, and a little ray of sunshine shone down on me at that moment. He stepped out of the RV shaking his lowered head, "Nope, I must have taken them out before we left for vacation." That sunny ray of sunshine disappeared. "The only thing I can tell you is to start pushing," was his answer to my dilemma. I looked at him as the rain ran off my helmet. I gave him the "are you kidding me" look. He says, "I have a piece of rope. I can tow you to a gas station."

You have to picture the situation and where this is taking place. This is a winding mountain road outside of Lake Placid, NY. There is nothing around for miles except hills, valleys, and "S" curves. I seriously considered the rope tow for a few seconds. Then I said, "Get the rope." I was in desperate need of a viable solution, and my choices were limited. I tied the rope to his back left bumper and through the forks onto my bike frame. He took off with me and my motorcycle in tow. If you are looking for some excitement in your life, try this. It's like waterskiing on a road. He started off slow enough but as we put a few miles behind us, he got more comfortable. HE GOT comfortable! His speed quickened as did my heartbeat. Around the wet curves, we traveled sometimes riding onto the gravel shoulder. Instinct told me to apply my brakes, but that did nothing to slow down his massive RV. "Hold steady," was my mantra, "Hold steady." My grip on the handlebars could have choked a horse.

We arrived twenty miles later at a small yellow gasless repair garage just north of Schroon Lake. I was trembling as I set the kickstand down on my motorcycle, grateful to still be alive. I untied the rope and thanked my tow man. An older gentleman emerged from the "man cave" wiping his hands with a greasy towel. "What seems to be the trouble young man?" "No power, nothing works," I replied. He, too, has a decent working knowledge of mechanical things after all, he runs this repair shop. He also has a dry garage. He removes the gas tank exposing the main electrical harness strapped to the frame. There, next to the frame, is an exposed wire. It wore through the insulation and shorted out. Some black electrical tape was applied; a new fuse and the gas tank replaced. "There, that should do it," he says. "Thank you so much," I said. "I have only two dollars left in my pocket. That's enough for gas to finish my trip home," I told him. "Aw, that's OK; I did my good deed for the day. You be careful out there." I was on my way again, and a little behind schedule. Half the day was spent on this little excursion. Monday morning work was getting closer, and time was running out. I made a promise.

The story doesn't end there. It is over forty years later. I live up in that same North Country not far from that old yellow garage. I can't drive past without recalling that infamous cold, windy, and rainy day. I recently stopped in. I wanted to see if the old man was still there; he's not. There was another man there, my age. It looked like he had the same greasy towel in his hands. I asked him about an older man back in the summer of '74. "Yeah, that's my dad," he says. I recalled the story of that day and how his dad repaired my motorcycle, for free. He smiled a broad smile. I told him how I didn't have any extra money to pay him. "Yep, that's my dad. He's gone now, and I run the place now." We shook hands as we both smiled. I looked up and gave thanks to a loving God, who was watching over me that day.

I still, occasionally, drive past that old yellow garage. I remember an old man taking the time-out to help a tired, frustrated motorcycle rider and asking nothing in return. Jesus said in Matthew 25, 'Assuredly, I say to you, inasmuch as you did it to one of the least of these My brethren, you did it to Me.'

I did not realize it then, but God sent a legion of angels to watch over that stretch of wet road and a cold rider, one who could have easily gone down on that cold, wet road. Oh yeah, I did make it to work, on time, Monday morning retelling the story of a crazy motorcycle tow ride on a mountain road to the old yellow garage.

Roadside Assistance

"You have not lived today until you have done something for someone who can never repay you."
—John Bunyan

When I left the college campus that rainy morning, I had little knowledge of what God had in store for me that day, most of us don't. We have no idea what is planned as we carry out our daily lives. We make lists, check them twice, and do our best to run our course. Whether it is a mechanical situation, another road warrior or just bad weather these obstacles cause delays. It is how we perceive and deal with them that make us different, somewhat better.

Road rage is the newest term these days. Short tempers and long lines are not good car mates.

Don't ride shotgun with a short-tempered driver. Our first reaction to an unexpected delay is to lash out in anger. God is usually on the other end. If we call on Him first, that helps us to stay focused on the immediate need for resolution.

Have you been stuck on the roadside? This motorcycle incident was not my first and not my last. What was your first reaction then? How did you get the issue resolved? Did you think about how God might have sent help without your knowledge? How would you react today under those same circumstances?

Both men in this story helped me out before they knew I could not repay them, yet, they didn't hesitate to help. Their hearts were open when my wallet wasn't. Today when I see someone stranded as I was, I think back to old yellow garage and a man with the greasy towel and smile.

Meditate on:

Much like a thick rope there are many strands giving it might. Untwist the strands and each on its own are easily broken. Its' strength comes from the help in the other strands coming together as one.

___

Pray on:

Lord, on my own I am unable to continue. You bring help to me in unusual ways that many times I do not recognize. Help me to see and understand Your helping hand in all I do. Amen.

Chapter 12

Pothole from God

"Life is full of detours and potholes. It is hard to know where God is leading us which is why trusting God is important."

Author unknown

I spend the bulk of my time behind the windshield of my Big Red Truck. I travel the roads of the nine states comprising the Northeast. What I do is not important to this story only that my time is spent driving. One recent trip took me to Long Island, NY. I visited places like, Babylon, Jericho, Mount Sinai, Bohemia, and Promised Land all without leaving the Island. I lived there once, years ago, in a different life, but that's another story. It has different names by those who live there and those who visit. Names like "Lawn Guyland," "Strong Island," and "Wrong Island" come to mind readily. For me, the real issue is getting there. They have ferries, tunnels and bridges and the elite would go so far as to take a plane or helicopter, mostly to avoid the "Road Warriors" like myself.

One of the routes to the "Island" is across the George Washington Bridge, GW. It connects Northern Jersey to upper Manhattan which you need to get over to the Throgs Necks Bridge then out onto the "Island." Not an easy trek for most. Me, I've done it a hundred times! After crossing the GW, you are automatically dumped onto the Cross Island Expressway. The name is deceiving; there is nothing express about this expressway! I have been traveling this road my whole life and cannot tell you when there hasn't been construction on this seven-mile stretch between the GW and the Throgs Neck Bridges.

I'm on the Expressway, left lane, heading for the Throgs Neck when "BAM!" I hit a pothole the size of Australia, and it wasn't one of those fake plastic ones either! I knew all too well this was not your ordinary variety pothole, this was a New York pothole. And the damage it installed would not be easily remedied. Coming up to the Throgs Neck

Bridge my dashboard lights up and that little, annoying "DING" starts chiming. We've all heard that little annoying "Ding" when you forget to fasten your seat belt, or your door is left open. The carmakers are sure to make that "DING" so annoying that you drop what you're doing and fix the infraction. "OK, OK," you say, "I'm getting there. Hold onto your horses!" You buckle up and "DING" suddenly disappears. "Whew," you say. "I can't take much more of that, that's for sure."

That little "DING" starts up. "DING" And it doesn't stop. "DING" One "DING" every second. "DING" The dashboard is flashing orange lights "DING" and messages on their new computer-based message center. "DING" Try driving in the worst traffic in the city with "DING" and lights and "DING." It doesn't stop – "DING." "Tire pressure too low." "DING" "Service Transmission" "DING." "Service Shifter" "DING." It doesn't stop! "DING" There is no way to stop it. "DING" Buckling up doesn't help. "DING" Opening and shutting your door doesn't help, nothing helps! "DING" You start praying, "Lord, help me." "DING" Traffic all around you. "DING" No one is letting you move over. "DING" No one can even hear the "DING," only you. "DING."

It's getting late and rush hour traffic is building, and I still have another hour to my first destination. I challenge anyone reading this to drive around the block without your seatbelt buckled, and you'll get a glimpse of "DING," unrelenting "DING."

I make it to my hotel for the night and get settled in. At least the "DING" has stopped, but it still "DINGS" in my head! The next morning brings silence from the dashboard. No orange lights and no "DING." Wow, maybe it corrected itself when I shut it off. Like most computers, these days rebooting them solves a lot of problems. Great, I can continue my trip in peace and quiet.

"DING," NAY, nay says the computer. I'm right back where I started. I look up a local truck dealership, and he is several miles away. I drive in and get the usual. "I'm booked up. I'll try to get to you before the end of the day." I find another dealer, and he gets to it right away and reports, "It was a computer problem. I needed to download a new upgrade, and it's all better. No charge, warranty." Wow – that was easy and cheap. Now we wouldn't have much of a story if that were the end of it. No, no says the computer! I pull out of the dealership and drive to the first traffic light. "DING" I make the quickest U-Turn ever and pull back in. I walk in, and the manager says, "This is not good." "No," says I, "it is not!"

They look at it again and tell me that they have to remove the whole computer system and check each circuit, and that's going to take days! I'm 400 miles from home, and the thought of driving back with "DING" does not excite me. I call the dealer I purchased the truck from back home. He says, "Bring it in here; I'll fix it, and if I can't fix it, I'll fix it so no one else can." The thought of driving five hours back through the Throgs Neck, the Cross Bronx Expressway and the GW with "DING" every second was more than I thought I could bear. I did some local work, and decided to head out the next morning.

"The Lawn Guyland Expressway" is not a pleasant road on a good day; now enter in "DING" every second. I purchased a set of those little orange sponge earplugs for the trip home. Any help I could get, I'd use. I started my sojourn home. As I was driving, I realized something strange, as I accelerated the "DING" stopped! The moment I decelerated it started up again. This was a new revelation; there was hope. All I needed to do was to continue to accelerate all the way home! There's the answer to my problem, sounded good at the time. The only problem was there were the other cars in front of me, and those pesky cars with the red and blue flashing lights behind me.

Here is where I said a prayer. "Lord, I know you have the power to fix this problem. This is nothing for you. If not, help me find the patience I need for this trip, Amen." Remember this prayer as we move further down the story.

As I'm driving, I can get a few seconds of silence as I accelerate up a small incline only to resume the "DING" on the downside. At least it was something. I had minimal control of the situation, and it wasn't going to beat me. God answered my prayer, well, almost.

I made it across the Throgs Neck Bridge onto the Cross Bronx and the GW, four more hours to go. As the drive wears on I'm noticing the speed of the acceleration is not keeping up with the silencing of "DING." I have to speed up on the inclines to stop the "DING." First, I was going 65 now I have to go 70. Then it went to 72.

I find myself traveling 74, 76, 78, and 80 just to keep the silence, if only for a couple of seconds. The silence is more than welcome. I have a busted head. Those earplugs – fuggedaboutit, useless. You only get funny looks from people you are passing as they see these bright orange plugs sticking out of your ears. 82 miles per hour, not a happy camper.

As I am approaching home, I call my dealership and notify him I am in the vicinity. He says, "Bring it in we'll wait for you so we can check it out." It's getting late, and they are about to close. I'm up to 84 miles per hour. I'm checking for red and blue lights behind me. I told the dealership it doesn't make the "DING" first thing in the morning, and you'll have to drive it around until it starts up again. "No problem, we'll look at it tonight for you." "Great, I'm almost there."

Remember that little prayer I said earlier in the day asking the Good Lord to fix the problem. Well, He answered my prayer, less than one mile from the dealership! I stopped at a light in town just short of pulling into the dealership and the "DING" stopped! "You've got to be kidding me!" I yelled out. I'm not making this up! Over five hours of "DING," and it stops less than one mile from the shop. I pulled in and told them it just stopped. You know that feeling when "That clanking sound" doesn't 'clank' for the repair guy. God does have a sense of humor, but this wasn't funny! I needed a "DING" and needed it

NOW! Where's the "DING?" He looked at it and told me to bring it in when I hear the "DING."

I did some math as I was driving home. The "DING" sounded once every second. Sixty "DINGS" every minute. Thirty-six hundred "DINGS" every hour. And 18,000 "DINGS" in the five-hour drive home. You can minus, maybe, 1000 for the up-hill acceleration that still leaves you with 17,000 "DINGS." I got one mile away, and it stopped! It was nerve-racking. The whole week was a disaster. What was God thinking? I have no idea. He knew what He was doing.

Philippians 4: 6-7, Paul speaks of following Jesus' example encouraging his followers to replace our anxieties with grateful prayer and trust. "Be anxious for nothing, but in everything by prayer and supplication, with thanksgiving, let your requests be made known to God, and the peace of God, which surpasses all understanding, will guard your hearts and minds through Christ Jesus.

I knew the Lord would watch over my situation. He created it and wanted me to trust Him, to have an inner calm or tranquility. I admit it was difficult during the drive home through some of the worst traffic. But believers in Christ can have peace in desperate situations. We have the assurance of the love of our heavenly Father. He cares for our needs as we bring them to Him with an attitude of thankfulness. As we trust Him, our true needs are met. He is in control.

P.S. They found and solved the problem several days later. A major electrical harness came loose, probably at the pothole. It was next to the air-conditioner motor rubbing the insulation off thus causing all the strange signals and that little "DING."

Roadside Assistance

"Where there is no struggle, there is no strength."
                                         Author Unknown

We live in a fallen world. No one can avoid every pothole in the road of life. Hard times are out there, and they will find you. There is no growth without tough times. Do not be dismayed. Do not hang your head low in shame, everyone has tough times. It is what you do with it that counts. When you say yes to God, it doesn't mean all will be well. There are lessons on the road of life to be learned. God is the best teacher. Recognize there is a lesson to be learned then contemplate what He is bringing to you.

Has there been a situation in your life where God was trying to get your attention? Did you see it as a hindrance or an opportunity? Did you shake your fist at the sky and scream, "Why me?" We fail in the heat of the moment to see Gods abundant grace.

We only see heartache and trouble. Have you ever slapped your forehead with the palm of your hand saying? "Now I get it!" That's the moment of growth. That's the moment God looks down and says, 'Ah HA, they got it."

When a weight lifter is in training, he is continually putting more weight on the bar to increase his strength. God does the same thing. When the bar gets too easy to lift, He puts more weight on the bar to increase your strength. Do you recognize it as God doing it? Do you drop the bar and say, "It's too heavy?" Know your strength is being tested and increased for something better, something bigger. God is standing as your spotter when you are going His way.

Meditate on:

The strength you will gain tomorrow is from the pain endured today. Each challenge you encounter has, in it, a buried opportunity for growth.

Pray on:

Lord, when I look in my rearview mirror I see pain, when I look ahead I am afraid, help me to look up and see You on the road ahead of me. Amen.

Chapter 13

Snow Angel

"As you travel life's road, Angels light the way and share the load."

Author unknown

The temperature was well below freezing and the wind was blowing the snow sideways. The plows couldn't keep up; the roads were covered. Visibility was less than a hundred feet. It was a white knuckle, face close to the windshield drive home from work. It was still light out; I left work early.

I got within five miles of my home. While stopped at a light at the Scotch Church intersection, I saw him. There, off to the right, outside the gate to the cemetery, he stood. His clothes were torn and ragged, and he sported a long gray beard. What was left of a hat sat atop his long, stringy gray hair. He held a yellow bag of groceries in his right hand. The closest grocery store was over fifteen miles away. Had he come that far? He looked across the intersection and our eyes met, sad, piercing eyes. I could see he was asking me, with those eyes, "Are you going my way?"

I slowly crept through the intersection. My old pickup truck did not have four-wheel-drive; I would slide sideways when I stepped on the gas too hard. I pulled over slightly. I'd never get my truck out of the ditch if I got too close. He looked through the passenger window and asked again with those eyes, "Are you going my way?" I motioned for him to climb in. It was obvious he hadn't seen a bathtub in some time. I asked him where he was heading. He mumbled, "Up the road a bit." I turned up the heat and blasted it on his feet. He had boots on, but they looked like George Washington handed them out.

As I came closer to my road, I was forced to ask again, "where are you going?" He told me he lived up on Fish House Road. It was well out of my way to my home, but I told him I would take him there; he could never walk it. I headed north then west through the blinding snowstorm. As I was heading down his road, he motioned to pull over. "This is where I live." "This is where you live?" I asked under my breath. Nobody lives in there! It was a large, worn down old barn. He thanked me, grabbed his yellow bag of groceries and stepped out into the blinding storm. I sat and watched as he made his way toward the old barn, each step dragging behind him. I said, "There is no way he lives in there." I drove on and found a suitable place to turn around. I drove slowly past the old barn to make sure he was safe. There were no footprints in the snow! There was no sight of "the man." Where did he go? How could he disappear so quickly? Was he real? Of course, he was real!

That little episode bothered me for some time. That night I came across Hebrews 13:2, "Be not forgetful to entertain strangers: for thereby some have entertained angels unawares." Was he sent as a test, as a messenger? I don't know. Was I going His way? I sure hope and pray I was going His way.

There is help even more astonishing. Our Creator-God descends into our daily life sees our needs and offers roadside assistance 24/7. Psalm 46:1, "God is…a very present help in trouble." Next time you feel stranded out there, on any road, look for your Helper, He's going your way.

Roadside Assistance

"Never drive faster than your guardian can fly."
Author unknown

We are visited by these heavenly beings regularly. God's love and grace are evident as He sends His messengers to visit and guide us. The message is not always clear at first. Sometimes years have to pass before we can fully understand the intended message. This meeting occurred over thirty years ago, and it has been with me ever since.

The Bible has angels mentioned 273 times, 108 times in the Old Testament and 165 times in the New Testament. The word "angel," comes from the Greek word *aggelos*, which means "messenger."

Countless artists have tried to capture their images through the years. The Bible describes angels differently than we might expect to see here.

Jesus was visited by guardian angels in the Garden of Gethsemane as well as Moses and many others in the Bible.

Not all angels are messengers. There are many unnamed angels appearing in Scripture, who carry out various responsibilities—all designed to serve God in one-way, or another. Messengers are on the top of the list. We know Gabriel. Following these messengers there are; guides, providers, worshipers, protectors, prayers answerers, strengtheners, deliverers, those caring for believers, executioners for sinners, including the Angel of Death.

My path crossed with an angel on that cold, snowy winter day. Has your path been crossed or interrupted by one of these heavenly beings? Did the phone ring as you were walking out the door making you late for an appointment, only to find there was an accident one minute earlier that could have been you?

Did you realize, at the time, who it was and why they called, maybe it was just a wrong number? You probably can't remember the who or why, but you can recall the near miss. How many times has God sent you a protector, prayer answerer, or guide? Did you stop, for a brief moment, and thank Him for loving you that much to take the time to care for you?

God does love you that much and wants to be sure the road you're on will get you to His place. Look out and look up.

Meditate on:

Whether a guest or host or a stranger ourselves, in any role we find ourselves we should be neighborly and charitable. This is so often hard for some to do. We show forth the love and charity which Christ has shown to us. One of these strangers is one chosen of God, an elect messenger who we have entertained unawares. You may never know who's life you effect, until that great day of the Lord

_____
_____
_____
_____

Pray on:

With meekness and fear help me show forth that Christian hospitality in brotherly love. Help me bring to mind and never forget to show hospitality to strangers!

_____
_____
_____
_____

Chapter 14

How Far is Far?

"God is never blind to your tears, never deaf to your prayers and never silent to your pain.
He sees, and He is never too far."

Author unknown

The company I was working for offered me a promotion. This involved moving, a huge road trip, the first of many. It was time to pick up, pack up and relocate, lock, stock, and barrel to another state. Moving across the "bridge" from the busy, city life to the country life was what the young family needed. To a five-year-old, who had become familiar to the life she was born into, this move seemed continental. It was hard for her to grasp that although her maiden homeland seemed light-years away, it was only seventy miles.

To this five-year-old and parents alike discussing the daily activities, at bedtime, had become a routine ritual. But it was one that was carried out with the utmost interest on both parts. We were settling into our new surroundings. We were all busy with a new home, new job, and other various relocation activities. A relocation road trip of this magnitude took most of our daily time. I did not realize that little time was given to a discussion about leaving Grandma and Pop-Pop back home. Not much is missed by a five-year-old. She quietly pondered if she would ever see them again.

On one particular evening, it was my turn to tuck her into the security of her white canopied bed. Her little world of sleep was not far-off; but, it had to wait. The question that was being pondered for awhile was finally asked, "Daddy, how far is far?"

I tried to explain as I looked into her curious eyes. But I found no reasonable answer that would satisfy the curiosity of this five-year-old. Not sure what she would be able to understand, after all, she just asked one of "those questions."

I kept my mouth shut; sometimes silence is best. I stared into her big brown eyes asking with my eyes, "are you serious?" I could see from her eyes, "yes – I want to know." As the Daddy, I tried to come up with the best answer to her question. I have known it is not polite to answer a question with a question, but I figured I'd give it a shot. So I asked, "Well, how far do you think far is?" She rolled her eyes heavenward with her hands folded behind her head paused for a moment. She looked into my eyes and said, "Far is when you yell and the echo doesn't come back." I asked her, "Is Grandma and Pop-Pop that far?" "No," she replied. She laid there and just smiled up at me. She turned over and fell fast asleep content she would never be far from them again.

A tear puddle in my eye knowing, yes, even five-year-olds can figure out answers to those questions parents stumble with at times. And, yes, I slept soundly that night too, knowing she will never be far from my heart.

Is God far from us? It sure seems that way sometimes. "Where are you God?" is the question we ask when fear sets in. God is not far; He is right where He always is, right next to us. Fear and sin keep us far from Him. God does not move we do. "Far is when you yell and the echo doesn't come back." Is God that far?

Roadside Assistance

"Distance – it's only as far apart as our hearts will let it.'
Author unknown

We see distance as a roadblock in life. Columbus, Lewis and Clark even NASA did not let distance get in their way of their goals. A marathon runner cannot see the finish line, yet he knows how far he must travel. The captain of a ship cannot see his next port of call, but he knows what needs to be done to reach his destination safely. One small man and one mammoth ship will eventually arrive at the final destination. He's been given the tools necessary to achieve this journey, and he knows how to use them.

We, too, have been given the necessary tools to arrive at our final destination. God has written it all down for us. Some 40 authors put God's words down on paper for us. God gave Moses Ten Commandments. They weren't suggestions or ideas; they were

COMMANDMENTS. God said you need to pay attention here; I'm not kidding. Do this or pay the consequences.

How many keep God at a distance because we don't know His rules? How far will we go before we stop Him? "If I go too far, then I have to change," is often a comment I hear. Ephesians 2:13 *"But now in Christ Jesus you who once were far-off have been brought nearby the blood of Christ."* Each sin we commit puts us farther away from God. Do you want to be that far from God? Do you want to be nearer to God? The choice is yours. God made the promise of heaven to be the driving force to keep us close to Him. How far do you want to be?

Meditate on:

God has done everything He can to provide you with what you need to be on His road. Don't waste any time running from Him or ignoring Him. Unconfessed sin will keep you from enjoying full fellowship with Him. All you have to do is accept Him.

_____
_____
_____
_____

Pray on:

Lord God, I confess that I have been wandering away from Your will and Your plan for my life, and I want to ask for your forgiveness. I want to refocus my life on You and to recommit myself to You. Though I have been far from You, please allow me to redirect my road towards You. I now want to reaffirm that commitment. Thank you for your forgiveness and for giving me your Holy Spirit. In Jesus name I pray, Amen"

_____
_____
_____
_____

Chapter 15

Good-Bye

"Treasured in my heart you'll stay until we meet again someday."

Author unknown

"Good-Bye," a phrase we heard and used at one time, or another. It can be heard at the end of a party, family reunions, business meetings, or church on Sunday mornings. You hear it at graduations. It has a special feeling of "so long for now" and "until we meet again." There are other times the "good-bye" phrase is not meant to be good at all, the close of a divorce hearing, or the slamming of the door just prior to such hearings. And the worse kind of "Good-Bye" is to a loved one leaving this life to move on to the next. This is the "Good-bye" I am most interested in right now. All the above "Good Byes" are a part of life and part ritual to help with many different ways of dealing with others in our lives.

There is a four-block cartoon, the kind you see in the daily newspaper. There Charlie Brown and Linus stand over a tree seedling. Charlie says to Linus; *"It's a beautiful little tree."* Linus responds with; *"Yes it is."* Charlie Brown says; *"Too bad we won't be around to see it when it's fully grown."* Linus gives him a puzzled look and asks; *"Why, where are we going?"* Like many teachers, they rarely get to see their students grow up and move out into the world. Linus has not figured out, he too, will not make it to the full lifetime of that little sapling.

Children and adults do not see life-and-death through the same eyes. We think they can see what we see. This is a mistake. As parents, we try to explain the best we can. Their life is a world of fantasy and imagination. They witness death regularly as reversible. They see characters dying and coming back to life again. This is not the real world. The only way a child comes to a more realistic view of death depends on how the parents deal with it.

The first teaching lesson opportunity comes with the ending of a child's pet. The struggle is at the beginning with the parent. They do not want to buy such a pet. They know what will eventually come to pass with the tears that will follow during the procession and burial. There is always the hope the pet thing will teach our children about life-and-death. It's about the deep attachments we make to other living things. It's just another ritual of hello and good-bye when we become attached to lives around us. It is also a simple lesson of existence. The pet story is also there to teach the child and sometimes the adult. It teaches about responsibility, affection, imagination, sorrow and death. You stand there over the small shoe box in the yard colored with crayons and little plastic flowers, reading "Good-Bye." This is not one of those good-bye for now, see you later kind of good-byes. This is for real and forever more.

My travels took me to a distant land recently. Not one across the "Pond," or to a foreign land. I just returned from Florida. No, it wasn't a vacation or business trip. This was one of those; I'm not quite sure how to explain it, kind of trips. My dearest older sister had terminal cancer. It was one of those trips. My sister, Roseann, found out she had cancer six months ago. She went through all the necessary treatments to ward off this nasty disease. The disease is winning. As I write this, Roseann lies in bed, surrounded by her husband, Dennis, my two youngest sisters, many friends and fellow believers. She is not the sister I knew – well – physically that is. She is a shell of the once healthy, vibrant, vocal big sister I knew. To sit next to her and hold her frail hand as she moves closer to God and His world I quietly recall all the times we had living.

She is an excellent cook, can make or fix anything, a knitter, crocheter, reader, painter, worshiper, hairdresser, wife, sister, teacher, evangelist and friend. She will remain to be all those when she gets to heaven. The first thing Roseann will do upon reaching the Pearly Gates is to give Saint Peter a haircut, he probably hasn't had one in years, and Roseann will tell him so, wherein everyone else in Heaven will get in line. She's a hairdresser by trade and untidy hair is inexcusable to her.

Eighty percent of people die in hospitals. If not at home, 911 is called and all the necessary agencies become, quickly, involved. Roseann is at home. Everyone knows what is to be done and knows his or her part in the ritual of death and mourning. But I don't want to continue talking about her death. My part in this surreal tragedy is to explain her life and her after-life. Roseann has a very strong faith in God, our God of the Bible. She knows what is on the other side and is waiting to go there. Her last words to me were simple. *"Frankie, I'm not suffering. I'm not in pain. I just want to go home. I love you."*

She might not have a clear understanding about life in heaven, but knows the promise of Jesus. Jesus told His disciples; *"The eye has not seen, nor has the ear heard or has it entered the imagination what my Father has prepared for you in Heaven."* She is not afraid of dying. It does not scare her. Nor does it scare me. You reevaluate your life as your mortality becomes more apparent. After witnessing her faith and strength in that bed, I was not there to say "Good-Bye," I was there to hold her hand and recall John 16:16. *"A little while, and you will not see Me; and again a little while, and you will see Me, because I go to the Father."* That was my ritual for "Good-bye." I love you too, Roseann.

When, your eyes see this; Roseann will be giving Saint Peter that, long overdue haircut. Her time here is short, but her time in Heaven is forever. She was picked up on this road of life and given her last ride to the front door of Heaven.

Roadside Assistance

"And God will wipe away every tear from their eyes; there shall be no more death, nor sorrow, nor crying."

Revelation 21:4

I miss my sister. She left me with wisdom to pass on, some is in this book. Death has touched everyone reading this in some way, or another and will again. Some are dealing with loss as they read this and wonder if they will get past it. I can't get through this story without tears myself. They say tears are 1% water and 99% feelings.

God sheds a tear every time one of His children is lost. He also rejoices when one of His children comes home to Him. The angels walk by your side into heaven, and Jesus stands there welcoming you. And that moment when the spirit sees God for the first time it will not see in the eyes of God anger and judgment and criticism, but the overwhelming love and tenderness and understanding and compassion, welcoming you home. *"Come – come into the Kingdom prepared for you from the beginning of time. I know your life was not easy. I know how much you fell. I know you fell many times, but I also know how much you cared for others and how many times you reached out to help others who were hurting and troubled and lonely and hungry. I know how much you cared, and I know how much you tried to love Me. So don't be afraid, welcome home."* And God embraces you with the love you never, never, dreamed possible and the joy and the rapture and the ecstasy that you experience is something far beyond our wildest dreams.

He continues to guide us, but our choices take us on different roads away from Him. What is the process you use for dealing with loss? Do you shutdown and hope it goes away? Do you lash out in anger to others, to God? Does dying scare you? We can never, never overestimate the understanding and compassion of God.

Meditate on:

Jesus intended the thought of heaven to be the most powerful motivating force in our life on earth capable of pulling us away from the enticing, appealing and material things around us. Heaven has to be the greatest possible thrill that we can ever experience. And heaven is not a place we should be afraid of. Dying is not something we should be afraid of. Seeing God is not something we should be afraid of. Is the road you're on going to get you to His place? Only you know. "Come, I've been waiting for you, your journey is complete."

_____

_____

Pray on:

Each night as I close my eyes, help me to think about that day, that moment, when I will be able to see You face-to-face. Help me to consider the joy, the thrill and the ecstasy of living in Your home, in the Kingdom of Heaven.

_____

_____

Epilogue

There are a couple of sayings I've heard through the years; "You are what you eat," "You are what you read," "The clothes make the man," and "You are what you drive." The health nut eats raw vegetables and juices to stay healthy while the over-weights down their doughnuts. The yuppie exec has the pinstripe suit, and the construction worker has jeans and boots. The young college grad drives his red sport convertible coup while his father drives his four-wheel drive pick-up and mom drives the minivan. See my point?

What is the process you use to filter out evil thoughts and consider only the good ones? Billy Graham once said: "I can't stop the birds from flying overhead, but I can keep them from nesting in my hair." At first the evil thoughts find their way into our everyday lives, but we do not have to entertain them. From a very early age, we are not taught to think; we are taught to remember, to memorize, and that is not the same as thinking. The word "mind," is mentioned 95 times in the Bible, but "brain" is not mentioned once. Our minds or consciences are involved with observations about the world around us. We constantly replay old conversations and past events, or we are busy rehearsing for those in our future. How we process all that information is crucial to our existence and growth.

Many people believe they can go about their lives on their own with no outside help. "I did it my way" are lyrics to a famous song teaching this concept. The Good Lord put each of us here with a purpose. If you were to view a sizable tapestry from the front, a colorful, detailed picture is clear, but if you were to see that same image from behind a different representation is viewed. It's a mess- tangled threads, some knotted, some long, some short, no particular order to it. God looks down on us and sees the finished tapestry from above; He sees and knows where each tiny thread is to be placed exactly and where it is needed to complete His picture. We, on the other hand, look up and see the backside of a tangled hodgepodge of string. It doesn't make any sense to us from our view. We see long strings, short pieces, some knotted, some hanging alone and we say, "I don't want to be that white piece over here by itself, I want to be over there with those other red pieces; I like those red pieces better." God's reply is, "I don't need you over there; I need you here to complete My masterpiece." This is the root of our discontentment with God. We are incapable of seeing from God's perspective. We rebel and turn our backs on Him. "God is not listening to me," we say. He sees the finished, completed picture while we only see the chaos from behind; it makes little sense to us. We will, someday, get to view that tapestry from above, and it is only then will we know how we fit into the big picture in God's tapestry. Meanwhile, we need to busy ourselves in staying where He put us to complete His plan.

How do we do this? How do we, as a piece of thread in God's design, complete His plan? We listen to God; we walk with God. Of all the individuals in the Bible, Enoch was one that stands out as having "walked with God." Enoch was 365 years old when he "was not." Enoch did not die; God took him to heaven one day. He was the prefigure of the Rapture to come. Genesis 5: 23-24 records, "And all the days of Enoch were three hundred sixty and five years. And Enoch walked faithfully with God; then he was no more, because God took him away." He was raptured into heaven, body, soul, and spirit by God. He was 360 years old when he decided to "walk" with God. Genesis 5:22 records: "And Enoch walked with God…three hundred years." Enoch separated himself from his current culture and made a decision to follow God.

A young girl, after Sunday School one day, was asked by her mother what she learned that day. She paused a moment and replied, "God came by Enoch's house every day and asked him to go for a walk. Enoch said, "Yes, let's go." One day God asked Enoch if he wanted to go for a longer walk; He had a lot to tell Enoch. Enoch said, "Yes." They started out for their walk and walked most of the day. After awhile, Enoch said to God, "It's late, shouldn't we turn back, we're pretty far from home." God said to Enoch, "You're closer to my home than you are to your home; why don't you come home with me?" He walked with God on earth and now he walks with God in heaven.

The Lord once said to His people, "Stand in the ways and see, and ask for the old paths, where the good way is, and walk in it; then you will find rest for your souls." God urged His people to look back so they could move ahead. The purpose of considering the ancient paths was to find "the good way" marked by God's faithfulness, His forgiveness, and His forward call. God can teach us from our past. The best road is the one we walk with Him. Let your past be a guidepost not a hitching post.

Some of you might remember John Denver, good singer and guitar player. One particular song he wrote some years back has a simple message, one that we can use to close this book. The song; "*Follow Me*" has the right sentiment for us to follow.

> *"Follow me where I go, what I do and who I know, make it part of you to be a part of me. Follow me up and down, all the way and all around, take my hand and say you'll follow me."*

Set your minds on things that are above, not on things that are on this earth. Be thankful for what God has provided. If you were to wake up with only what you thanked God for yesterday, what would you have today? There is so much to be thankful for; if you don't believe that, go back and reread "Problem or Inconvenience."

We are what we choose to be by the decisions we make. Our output is a direct reflection on our in-put. Sir Isaac Newton gave us the law of "Cause and Effect;" good cause-good effect, bad cause-bad effect, and no cause-no effect. You are the sum total of your thoughts; you become what you think about.

Someone once asked me, "How much can I get away with and still go to heaven?" The answer was simple, "Is what you're doing pleasing to God? Is it pleasing to you and others or pleasing to God?" The answer is simple, but the decision is rarely simple.

"The Beginning"

www.ingramcontent.com/pod-product-compliance
Lightning Source LLC
Chambersburg PA
CBHW052037070526
44584CB00016B/2079